ADVENTURING WITH CHRIST

SPECIAL LIMITED
COMMEMORATIVE
EDITION
1st published,
London, England
— 1938 —

ADVENTURING WITH CHRIST

*The Triumphant Experiences of
Two Men of God Around the World*

By
LESTER F. SUMRALL

"The Lord God omnipotent reigneth."
—*Revelation 19:6*

LeSEA PUBLISHING CO.
SOUTH BEND, INDIANA

Unless otherwise indicated,
all Scripture quotations are taken from
the *King James Version* of the Bible.

ISBN 0-937580-39-2
Reprinted 1988
Published by LeSEA Publishing Company
P.O. Box 12
South Bend, Indiana 46624

CONTENTS

FOREWORD

INTRODUCTION OF THE
1938 EDITION

WHY this volume, after ancient King Solomon predicted that of the making of books there was no end? There are two reasons:

Firstly, while meditating before God upon the subject, I sought to drop the matter, but it continued to weigh heavy on my soul. Therefore, in harmony with the divine impulse, I began to write the manuscript.

Secondly, a great desire burned within to place another story of modern miracles before a skeptical world.

I would that Christendom, and especially the young folk of this generation, could catch the vision of John, as he was exiled away on Patmos desert strand; and see the Almighty God, high and lifted up, surrounded by an innumerable host of Holy Beings, singing the Hallelujah Chorus, because the Lord God Omnipotent Reigneth! Not DID reign in the past, or WILL reign in the future—but REIGNS in the marvelous present!

I am happy that I believe and have experienced

that our Redeemer truly liveth! Not that by my unbelief could I remove the Sovereign of the Universe from His resplendent throne of glory, dignity and power; but by my believing it, I am the unworthy recipient of every needed blessing from the tender hands of an eternal Potentate.

I could easily believe, from the trend of modern life, that Christianity is on the threshold of a new era; it will either go forth in a mighty spiritual crusade against sin and the devil, believing and practising all the cardinal truths of the Bible, or continue to corrupt within and disintegrate and go into oblivion.

To me it seems that the work of the explorer has been triumphantly finished. As a result of the spirit of adventure, thirst for knowledge, desire for fortune or fame, we have not only the geography of the world, but have become largely acquainted with its civilization and life. Our generation is the first with such a marvelous world-wide scope. I believe this to be the greatest challenge ever thrown into the ranks of the Christian Church, and the supreme opportunity to fulfil the Great Commission!

L.F.S.

ADVENTURING WITH CHRIST

INTRODUCTION TO THE 1988 EDITION

*T*HIS special commemorative edition of *Adventuring With Christ* is being issued in honor of Dr. Lester Sumrall's seventy-fifth birthday. This volume, first published in England and America fifty years ago, is Brother Sumrall's account of his first missionary journey which took him around the world. The primitive conditions and means of travel of half a century ago did not stop or hinder Lester Sumrall and his mentor Dr. Howard Carter as they ventured with Christ through the down-under, the wonderous Orient, the forbidden heights of the Tibetan Himalayas, the frozen waste lands of Siberia and Nazi-dominated Europe.

You will thrill to the account of God's provision and direction in this around-the-world miracle journey. After reading this introductory testimonial, you will certainly wish to read other of Lester Sumrall's biographical works detailing his ministry and missionary experiences. May we suggest **Run With The Vision** or **My Story For His Glory.**

Today at 75 years of age, Lester Sumrall is still adventuring around the world for Christ. As a leader in mass-media evangelism, Lester Sumrall has published over 100 books. He also operates four Christian television stations, one local FM radio station and a dual-antenna shortwave station operating 24-hours daily into South America, Europe, North Africa, the middle East and the communist bloc nations. His television programs, including LeSEA Alive, The Lester Sumrall Teaching Series, and numerous specials are aired through the PTL, TBN and LeSEA satellite networks in addition to numerous individual television stations at home and abroad.

Lester Sumrall's missionary zeal has taken him to over one hundred nations to minister. The churches which he has established are still flourishing in such places as the Philippines and Hong Kong. Manila Bethel Temple Cathedral of Praise, seating 10,000, is one of the largest Christian churches in the Orient. At home in South Bend, IN, Dr. Sumrall pastors the Christian Center Cathedral of Praise and serves as president of World Harvest Bible College. A busy evangelistic schedule takes this preacher to every corner of the U.S. and the world each year. Rev. Sumrall also hosts annual tours to the Holy Land and the mission field.

After fifty-eight years in the ministry, Dr. Lester Sumrall is still *Adventuring With Christ*.

Chapter 1

HOW THE MISSIONARY JOURNEY ORIGINATED

IT was in one of London's grey stone churches, that a minister was engaged in a day of prayer. After a few hours' meditation, the Holy Spirit moved upon him in prophetical utterance, saying, "Arise, thou my servant, and prepare for the journey; let not another send thee, for I shall send thee and supply all thy needs. Arise, and go, be a blessing to my people in the uttermost parts of the earth."

From that moment, Mr. Howard Carter began preparing for a tour that had no mapped itineraries. The first part of the tour brought him to America. Here he spoke at large camp meetings, and in some of the largest churches in the United States.

While serving as a main speaker at a nationally represented camp meeting in Eureka Springs, Arkansas, a young American met him and felt that he also would like to venture by faith around the world. As they were conversing together, to the astonishment of both, Mr. Carter found that this young man fulfilled a sure word of prophecy given him by the Lord some four years before. This young man is the writer of the narrative.

From these providential happenings sprung one of the greatest triumphs of faith known to this generation. Two men started out with no financial resources and traveled around the globe. Mr. Carter, a strict keeper of statistics, estimates that we traveled, on an average, a thousand miles a week, while we were on our tour. We asked nothing of anyone, but received with gladness whatever the Lord was pleased to send.

Twenty-one different means of conveyance were used. We rode nearly everything there is to ride: passenger bicycle, three-wheel taxies, sedan chairs carried by natives, mule back for nine weeks on one journey averaging the "stupendous" speed of three miles per hour! In addition we made a few thousand miles in most luxurious airplanes averaging the "monotonous" speed of three miles per minute. We rode camels, donkeys, springless carts, and luxurious ships of the deep.

We preached in eighteen foreign languages with the help of sixty-five interpreters.

These experiences led us to the fascinating copper-colored Polynesians of Oceania, to the wide open spaces of Australia, to the beautiful Malayans of Java, to primitive tribes near Tibet, and mountains of Burma, to China's despondent millions, and to the keen, progressive Japanese in his magnificent island home.

We saw exile camps in Siberia, and the fury of Red Russia, where you payed five dollars gold for an ordinary meal.

We visited the peaceful and polite, flaxen-haired Scandinavians and our kindred countries of England, Wales, Ireland, and Scotland, ending the tour by visiting our friendly neighbor, Canada.

As the dim, misty panorama moves before him, the writer feels that if only he could live as long as Methuselah, with the patience of Job, the faith of Abraham, the bravery of David, and with the purity of Christ, he might come to understand the mystery of it all—then die content, having been a blessing to mankind.

The challenge that I feel is facing Christianity is that if she does not arise with Apostolic power and go forth to conquer the people and religions of the world, they in turn will come to our shores, animated with the powers of darkness, and subdue us, as eastern cults are striving to do at present.

Standing in the White Russian railway station in Moscow, I read a local newspaper written in English. A young leader of the youth movement, after outlining their activities against religion, morality, the home, etc., concluded his article by stating that "We young Communists of Russia will live for Communism and we will die for Communism!"

This rash decision sent a wave of holy indignation over my being. If these supposedly intelligent people will live for godless, immoral, insane Communism, and die for it—how much more should the followers of the Immaculate Prince of Glory live for Him and, by His all-sufficient grace, offer their bodies as a sacrifice to His worthy cause!

Oh! That Christendom again could give birth to some mighty men, "for such a time as this," who would catch the faith of Hudson Taylor, the zeal of Livingstone and the perseverance of Judson, to wing this eternal soul-saving message to the ends of the earth!

Hallelujah! The Lord God Omnipotent Reigneth!

CHAPTER 2

PROVIDENCE

THE night was majestic, and the starry city of God was lustrous above us. The R.M.S. *Makura* was slightly pitching as she plowed through the mysterious deep of the North Pacific. Below were the silvery waves, splashing against our trustworthy vessel, while my face was being bathed in briny mist.

I was standing in the very bow of the steamer all alone, gazing into the wondrous blue vault of heaven. Becoming retrospective, I lost sight of my environment and was carried away in thought, concerning the last few weeks of my life.

As we were speeding toward the point where nautical miles become shorter (equator), I opened my "book of reminiscenes" and began to soliloquize.

Mystery! Wonder! Providence! Here I was on my way to Australia, to meet and travel around the world with a man I had only met once. How strange! When Mr. Carter and I met in Eureka Springs, Arkansas, God made it very definite to us both by a prophetic utterance given to Mr. Carter, that we were to travel together.

While I was getting a passport from the Department of State in Washington, D.C., my newly discovered companion was fulfilling some speaking engagements in Australia. We planned meeting again in Hong Kong, China.

I had bought my ticket, had some luggage placed on the boat, and had been requested to speak at the divine services on Sunday while at sea. Only two more days, and I would be on the high seas; and then I received a special letter from Mr. Carter, saying, "Don't sail for China. Come to Australia. New developments have changed our itinerary. An invitation to Java for two months also open doors in New Zealand."

What could I do? Steamship companies do not refund money at a moment's notice, and I had no money for another ticket. Sitting in the city square of San Francisco, I prayed for divine assistance, then went to the office where I had purchased my ticket, and laid the difficulty before the clerk.

He replied, "I can do nothing. Matters of this kind are handled through our Chicago office."

"But, sir, I need my money today," I answered.

He scowled. "Yes, and I could have sold this cabin a dozen times, if I had known this."

"Please see what you can do about it," I pleaded.

"Let me speak to my manager," he said, as he walked into a private office with my ticket.

Soon the clerk returned and said, "The manager

has decided to refund your money." I inwardly shouted, "Hallelujah! For our Lord God Omnipotent Reigneth!"

Two days later, I was walking up the gang-plank of a steamer bound for Australia. As she slowly pushed away from the dock, breaking the colored streamers, I waved farewell to Mr. Craig, the founder of the great Glad Tidings Temple and Bible Institute of San Francisco, and his students. Soon we passed the famous Devil's Island Prison, and through the Golden Gate into an unknown world for me. Here I was at sea, starting around the world adventuring with Christ.

No society or church was sending us. No one was sponsoring the tour financially. Someone says, Well, what was your financial reserve! Twelve dollars!—that is, in English money, about £2.8s.

I had resolved that if God could feed Elijah by the brook Cherith, he could supply our needs. Thus we set forth trusting to be a blessing to Christians everywhere.

Chapter 3

UNDER THE SOUTHERN CROSS

IT was evening. Our steamer had followed the irregular coast line of the North Island all day. On the morrow we should be in Wellington, New Zealand.

As the southern skies became luminous, putting on her scintillating night-cap of indigo, set with the gems of paradise, my eyes scanned the heavens looking for the "glowing cross." There it was—the same majestic, blazing, constellation which, scientists say, 5,000 years ago entranced the old world, but which now is completely hidden from the Northern Hemisphere!

Surely, the fool hath said in his heart, "There is no God;" but the wise man said the heavens declared the glory of God.

The morning came, and we awoke to find ourselves surrounded by civilization and lying at anchor in a harbor. It was "windy" Wellington—the city set on a hill, the seat of modern civilization of New Zealand. Here the Wellington settlers came in 1840.

My emotions were stirred as I beheld the place where Henry Williams landed in 1823, as the first missionary to the aborigines in this island. Less than a century ago, this beautiful land of geysers and eternal snow-clad mountains was a synonym for savage barbarism, but the Gospel has the same marvelous transforming power in a wilderness of savagery, as in a rich metropolis.

I was only in New Zealand for thirty-six hours, but Mr. Howard Carter was there for a few weeks, visiting every large city, conducting Bible conventions, stirring up a new faith and zeal for another world-wide visitation from God among his compatriots who are living so far away from their native Britain.

It was four-thirty in the morning. I turned on my bunk with a trace of weariness, and a great desire to reach my destination. Twenty-four days of continuous sea life is a little too much for one's first voyage.

As I gazed out of the port-hole, I saw lights flickering in the distance. Going on deck, where the beautiful stars were shining above, and the sea rippling beneath, I beheld the magnificent God-designed harbor of Sydney. It is dotted with islets, each of which had flashing lights of warning to passing mariners. One would never fancy this paradise to have been at one time a penal dumping ground for Britain's criminals.

As we came into the harbor, we had picked up the pilot, State doctor and emigration officers from the motor-launch in which they had met us. All passengers had been given declaration forms to fill out, which contained questions regarding nationality, occupation, and other similar matters. One of the questions was—"How much money have you?" and underneath were added the words, "If you are a foreigner staying in Australia three months, you must have £200." Two hundred pounds! I left the space blank and went in before the emigration officer.

A young American was just in line ahead of me, and I overheard the conversation between him and the immigration officer, who with a loud voice said, "Seventy-five dollars!" "Yes, sir, that is all." "We do not want beggars in Australia, we want tourists with money." "Well, that is all I have." "Give me your passport and ticket; we are going to send you back to America on the next boat!"

I was the next to meet the officer. Reticently I laid my declaration form before him, and he glanced over it. "An American, eh?" "Yes, free born." "A minister, huh?" "Yes, of religion." "Say, there is one of the questions you have not answered," and taking his fountain pen, he said, "I will fill it in for you. How much money have you?" "I haven't very much." Looking up sharply, he said, "I did not ask you that question. How *much* money have you?" "Well, I really do not have very much." I was thinking that if having

$75.00 would get a fellow sent home, well, $12.00 would certainly seal my fate. Smiling as best I could under such circumstances, I softly said, "My present reserve is a bit short, sir." He then asked me, "Where are you going from here?" Receiving an inspiration I said, "I am going around the world, to preach the Gospel to those that have never accepted Christ as their Savior. I am going to Java, Singapore, China, Manchuria, Korea, Japan, and the Lord will provide." With this the officer went to fetch the Chief Inspector, while I prayed silently. I was again questioned on similar lines, at the end of which the inspector looked at me for a moment in silence, then said, "We are going to let you land." From his presence I went singing hallelujah! Our God Omnipotent is on the throne.

My first invitation to speak was in Melbourne, and on my arrival there at noon the following day, I was met by Mr. Greenwood, Pastor of Richmond Temple, and given a hearty welcome to Australia. After a couple of nights of fellowship with the Melbourne Christians, I was invited to visit Bendigo, a city about a hundred miles from Melbourne. Here I came to realize that I needed some local currency, so I prayed definitely for £5. After prayer the first man I met said that he and his wife felt impressed while at prayer to give me a gift. When I returned to my room I opened the envelope which they had given me, and there was—yes, my five pounds. Holding it in my hand, I thanked and praised my Omnipotent God of Love.

On returning to Melbourne, I found a letter from Mr. Howard Carter telling me to join him in Sydney and then we would proceed to Queensland and on around the world together.

I had sufficient money for a ticket, but, during my morning devotions, I was impressed to pray for a ticket to Sydney. I prayed until I felt the assurance that it would come.

At noon, as I was sitting at the table with my Scottish host and family, a man came in. "Mr. Sumrall, are you going to Sydney?" "Yes, on the three o'clock express." "Well, I have a ticket for you." Upon seeing the ticket, I was overjoyed, and in my heart I sang again, Hallelujah! Our Almighty God is still on the throne.

Arriving in Sydney the following morning, I was met by Mr. Duncan, the pastor of Jubilee Temple. During the next few days there were gracious outpourings of blessing in the meetings. Sinners were converted, and Christians revived. The Watch Night service on December 31st proved to be a special time of refreshing, God's children looking forward into the unknown future of the New Year with renewed zeal and faith for another mighty Pentecostal outpouring.

On the first day of the year, at ten-thirty a.m., I watched the beautiful white S.S. *Maraposa* as she gracefully steamed into the harbor and docked at her wharf.

With longing eyes, I scanned her crowded deck, but all in vain. Then, in the customs shed, I accidently came face to face with Brother Carter. Giving vent to my emotions, I heartily embraced him before all. It had now been five months since the Lord had so miraculously brought us together in His Providence, and for His work. From Sydney we now hoped to launch forward with one heart and aim, to trust God for protection, finance, and greatest of all, precious souls for His Kingdom.

While waiting for our boat to sail north, we had a few days to minister to different churches in the vicinity. Heaven's blessings were ever present. In the aftermeetings, while waiting on God, some were filled with the fulness of the Holy Ghost.

Leaving Sydney, we sailed by the S.S. *Morella* for Queensland. On January 7th, about five p.m., our ship steamed into Moreton Bay, and later into the beautiful Brisbane River.

We arrived in Brisbane in the midst of her torrid January heat. A few Christians were down at the dock to greet us. They heartily assured us a great welcome awaited us in the North.

The same day we journeyed up in the mountains about a hundred miles, to Toowoomba, to meet Mr. Charles Enticknap, the President of the Assemblies of God in Queensland. Two nights were spent in meetings there. The Australian enthusiasm was marked. The infilling of the Holy Spirit was experienced by a number of souls during these two days. It was wonderful to feel the nearness of our blessed Savior as we worshiped, as foreigners in the flesh, but with true consanguinity in the Spirit.

Mr. Carter began a tour of most all the cities in Northern Queensland, while I was given the task of conducting a tent campaign in Brisbane. We erected the "Canvas Tabernacle" by faith that all needs would be supplied, and began to fight the power of sin. From the first night, souls found God at the old-time altar, in the old-time way.

The Communists were very bitter against the tent revival. They came almost every night, but stood on the outside. If world conditions were stressed and especially Russia, they would nearly go wild with rage. While they were heckling one night, I commented that if you talked about the devil his children got angry. They stopped and went home for the night!

Near the close of the campaign, a young man rushed upon the platform one night. His face was pale and the very picture of anguish. At first, I thought he wanted to fight, or cause a disturbance, but when tears began flowing, I knew he was under a deep conviction of sin. He knelt and prayed until peace came to his wrecked soul. On rising to his feet, he said, "Last night, I was so angry I determined to burn this tent, but an unknown power constrained me. Praise God, now I am saved!"

God also marvelously healed many afflicted bodies. Among them was a man who had had an internal pain in his back and side for years. He said that if God would heal him he would serve Him. I said, "All right, it is a contract." We prayed, and I said, "The pains are gone, are they not?" "Well I do feel easy now, but my pain will return when I lay down to sleep." I replied, "Oh, no, you are sleeping tonight without pain." The following night, as I walked into the tent, he met me, and at first I did not recognize him; his features were changed. He was wearing a broad smile. His first words were, "Preacher, I am healed! I have not had a pain in my body since last night."

A certain young lady had a painful sore on the inside of her nostrils. One night she came to the meeting and said the sore had eaten through to the outside of her nose. Removing a small piece of cotton-wool, she showed me a terrifying cancerous sore, and said that the doctor was going to operate on it. I said, "Let the Great Physician do the operating. He does not use knives." We prayed for her, and in a few nights she came back with a bright testimony of healing.

Mr. Carter now arrived back from the north, and the purpose for coming to Queensland could begin, namely, the opening of a Bible school for preparing the young Christians of Australia for the ministry. The school opened with great joy, many of the "fathers and mothers in Israel" saying, "This day hath God answered our prayer."

As it was exceedingly hot, the classes were held under a marquee in a large park. Students from all parts of Australia were present on the opening day.

What memories linger concerning this wonderful open-air school! How keen were these men and women to get a deeper understanding of God's Word.

When the students were ploughing their way through a difficult problem, Mr. Carter's voice could be heard saying, "My maxim is, 'There is no royal road to success.' But success comes by perseverance and hard work."

Just in the solemnity of a lecture someone would roar with laughter outside. Then probably four or five others would follow suit—Ha, Ha, Ha-higher and higher. What was it? Then a native would say, "It is the laughing jackass." This bird imitates human laughter almost to perfection. Usually when one of them throws his head back and laughs, a group follows in rhythmical pursuit. Next all the Bible School pupils followed with a hearty laugh. This broke the strain of study.

The school was such a marked success in its four week summer session that a building was secured in the city to continue it after Mr. Carter and I were gone. An efficient staff of teachers were secured, the principal, Mr. Wiggins, coming out from England to take charge of it. The school has since been moved to Toowoomba, the Garden City of Queensland.

We found the Australians to be second to none when it comes to welcome feasts and farewell teas. The night before we sailed for Java, the ladies of the church prepared a "farewell tea" for us. As the Christian friends gathered around the table singing songs of Zion and praises to God, it seemed to kindle again that homesick feeling in our hearts for the Great Marriage Supper of the Lamb, when we all shall sit together singing praises to our heavenly Bridegroom, never to be parted any more, but to enter into His Kingdom to dwell in bliss for evermore.

Chapter 4

IN JAVA

ON March 9th, a number of our newly-made Australian friends came down to the wharf to see us off to Java.

At nine-thirty p.m. the gang-plank was lifted, and a harbor tug-boat gently pulled the steamer away from her mooring. The paper streamers were soon broken, and the words, "God be with you till we meet again," sung by our Pentecostal friends, grew fainter as we moved slowly down the Brisbane River and into the Coral Sea, for a fifteen day journey to Java.

The rising sun made the Java sea glimmer like gold. With our heads protruding through a port-hole, we saw a beautiful sight. The complete seascape was dotted with hundreds of sail boats. Their sails were outspread in the wind and they were gliding swiftly toward us. We were approaching the Javanese fishing grounds.

At ten-thirty a.m. the *Morella* threw her steel hawsers to the dock, and we were soon tied up in Sourabaya, an East Indian port. For the first time we were facing the Oriental in his homeland. For the next two months we were to travel the length and breadth of their island home, which has about the same area as England, and claims to be the most densely populated section on the globe. One hundred and forty-five million are living on a strip of *terra firma* only six hundred and sixty miles from tip to tip. This strange little island has fifty volcanic mountains. Four of these are active, belching smoke, growling internally, and sometimes hurling stones of death through the mouth of the crater.

As soon as the gang-way was lowered, Mr. and Mrs. Van Abkoude, our hosts while in Java, came on board. Although, we had never met before, the hall mark of salvation was sufficient recognition; we greeted each other without any formal introduction. Our baggage was soon past the customs, and we were taken to our room to prepare for the meetings in Sourabaya.

I think Sourabaya must be one of the most torrid, humid cities in the world. We were nearly prostrated before the sun went down. In Java the season never changes. It is a land of perpetual summer, where flowers never cease to bloom, trees ever put forth new leaves, and birds chirp in the tropical undergrowth. You see monkeys playing through the trees and across the road, looking at you from their hiding place behind a large banana leaf.

In the evening our friends called to take us to our first meeting in Java. Arriving at the church, we found the large concrete auditorium, which seated 1,200 people, filled to capacity, people standing around the walls and in the aisles. It was estimated that there were 2,000 people present. As we entered, the Javanese choir was singing. Not one word could we understand; but as they sang the songs of Zion with fervor, and the Hallelujah Chorus to perfection, the strangeness of their beautiful language disappeared and our souls caught the same spirit of praise.

The pastor asked Brother Carter to speak first. His message was interpreted into Malayan, this being the street language, or the common one which the Dutch, Chinese, Malayanese, Javanese and English alike could understand. We both prayed that in spite of the "curse of Babel," which caused us to need an interpreter, that God would anoint the two speakers with His Spirit; also, that all racial distinction would be lost at the Cross.

After Brother Carter had spoken, I was asked to give an evangelistic message. When the appeal was given for the unsaved, a great number came forward. It was a wonderful sight to see the different nationalities kneeling at one altar, praying to the one and only God.

The next morning we went for a walk and saw many interesting sights. It interested us to see hundreds of Pikolans, "walking restaurants." A native takes a long bamboo pole, which goes over his shoulder, then on each end he places the goods that he sells. He just stops in all the dust and grime of a crowded street, sits down on the curb-stone, lights his little charcoal stove which he generally carries on one end of his pole, and cooks your food that maybe you have ordered from him. When he has finished cooking, down the crowded street he goes shouting at the top of his voice for another customer. Another novelty that attracted our attention was the Demo "three-wheel taxi." It looks like a great tricycle with a cab built on. Desiring to return to our lodging place, we hailed a Demo and so had our first ride in one.

The following evening we had another great meeting. The Lord blessed us in a marvelous way, many sinners making confession of salvation, while Christians were driven to a deeper consecration in God, some receiving a definite infilling of the Holy Spirit.

After Sourabaya, our next place to speak was Magelang in Central Java, in the church of Mr. Van Abkoude, our host and Chairman of the Assemblies of God in Dutch East Indies. The meetings were well attended, and blessing flowed from the Fount of God. Conversions and baptisms were recorded in the annals of the Book of Life. Our interpreters being Dutch, they did not always understand our English idioms in speaking. At times they would say, "That will not translate," or on another occasion we would be telling a thrilling story, with fervor, only to be interrupted in the middle with, "Vot, Brudder, vot you say, Brudder?"

Traveling from Magelang to Blabok, we held a meeting for deeper spiritual life in the latter place. The Christians gathered together with hungry hearts, seeking the eternal Bread of Life. Then through tropical forests; by native villages where often one saw sad sights. Here was a poor old woman eaten up by leprosy with the pores of her skin a solid mass of running cancers, her nose eaten completely off, and eyes eaten out, with fingers ready to fall off, and a small boy leading her as they begged for a penny to buy food.

At Samarang, one of the leading seaports of Java, we had meetings with Mr. and Mrs. Able in their mission hall. Large crowds came, Dutch, Javanese, Malayanese, Chinese, all seeking to find the Prince of Peace. This being one of the important centers, Mr. Van Abkoude secured the large Masonic Temple auditorium for a city-wide mission. This venture was greatly blessed of God, the throngs hearing the Gospel story of the risen Savior.

From Samarang we crossed to the eastern part of the island, speaking in Solo (or Surakarta), the quaint city where one of the two remaining Sultans lives in his grand palace. The means of conveyance here were antiquated buggies, pulled by two small ponies, the size of the well-known Shetland kind. In this dreamy island town, so old and Oriental, we saw our first Javanese drama or shadow play. It was really a novelty. A great crowd stood around the entertainer. He had in his hand a long grotesque-looking leather doll. With a lighted lantern he threw its shadow on a screen. As he moved it about, to the music of the gamelon (Java's favorite musical instrument), he chanted a weird story of some of Java's demi-god warriors who lived long ago. The shadow play was the means of the first Christian revival of Java. Missionaries did not seem able to interest the quaint little copper-colored Javanese. A missionary of Russian descent came and he bought one of these dolls and sat on the sidewalk making it perform while he told wonderful stories, such as David and his triumphant victory over Goliath, Jonathan and his armorbearer defeating a whole army, and how brave Esther won the King's heart and saved a nation. Last of all he told of the Savior and His sacrifice, and hundreds believed and were converted. Praise God!

Leaving Solo, we preached in Madiun and then on to Kediri. Here we spoke for Miss Alt, a faithful and tireless warrior for God for over twenty years in Java. The mission hall was decorated most beautifully with flowers and tropical foliage, with a large sign over the pulpit, saying, "Welcome, Brudders Carter and Sumrall to Kediri." The hall was packed. We enjoyed the spontaneous, joyful singing of these happy folk. It made us feel welcome. The mission hall being too small, Sister Alt secured a large theatre building, and it was packed to the doors, with many outside. Needless to say, the Gospel net dragged in the fish from the Sea of Souls.

In this meeting the native children presented a play. Dressing like different nationalities, they each told what Christ had done for them. The South Sea cannibal had laid aside his spear and does not now eat human flesh, while the Chinese laid aside superstition and idols, etc. The natural gift for acting inbred in the Javanese made their drama very impressive.

Departing from Kediri we preached in Probolinggo and Malang. The church here seemed very progressive. The professor of a Dutch College was the band and choir master. The native singing was beautiful. One of the leading members of the congregation was a Javanese magistrate, a private counsellor to the Sultan. He was a large dignified gentleman wearing a many-colored skirt and a little turban. He made me a present of a sarong and turban when I was leaving.

The eastern friends surely believe in extravagant decorations for special occasions. They even rewhitewashed the walls of their mission, writing our welcome in large black letters; and there were flowers everywhere. The more we saw of these entrancing little people the more endeared they became to our hearts.

Now we were off to Temonggoeng, where meetings had been announced. A good representation of villagers were out to see and hear these men who talked in a strange language, while, to their surprise, their pastor interpreted it to them!

The banker of Temonggoeng desired to take us to see a volcanic mountain and show us a live crater. Having never seen one, we were pleased to go. Starting at four o'clock in the morning, we drove twenty-five miles in his car, and then the road ended. Here we found about a dozen Javanese boys with horses for hire. We had one each to take our party up the great Dieng, a very high mountain range in Central Java.

By eleven o'clock our strong little mountain ponies had us on the summit of the Dieng, where you can look south into the Indian Ocean, and north into the Java Sea. We soon descended into the old crater abyss that had erupted and burst the mountain into sections. In the center we saw the large sulphur springs, vomiting a nauseous cloud of smoke, and about a dozen small springs bubbling up a muddy substance. By putting your finger to the ground, you find you are walking on beds of fire.

While eating lunch, our friend said, "Would you like to see Death Valley?" Our curiosity was immediately aroused; the answer was in the affirmative. Therefore, down the mountainside we rode and over a small ridge. In an hour our guide said we were nearing Death Valley. We made a turn in the road and a sign-post met our eyes. It nearly made the blood curdle in our veins. All it had on it was a cross-bone and skull, with an arrow pointing to the valley. In a few moments the horses could go no further, so we dismounted and walked on.

We came to an incline with about fifty steps that had to be climbed in order to look down into this valley of death. At the foot of the steps we saw a large tombstone and inquired why it should be placed in such a wilderness. Our Dutch friend interpreted the writing, and the story said a German scientist came and looked at the valley but did not believe death was in it, and he descended with a rope tied around him. He was pulled back by his Javanese servant a dead man. His mother requested that he be buried there as a warning to others who come to see the valley.

We ascended the steep incline until we met a sign, "DANGER! Stop! do not go further." We obeyed the sign. Now we could see all the tropical forestry. It looked as peaceful and harmless as any valley in the world, but any animal or human who descended into its woeful depths never lived to tell the story. Scientists have explained that poisonous gases exude from the ground, and are so powerful that they instantly take life.

As our sturdy ponies took us back to the car, I thought of Death Valley, and how it resembled sin. Those enchanting, enticing, death valleys of the devil. Oh, that sinners could see the memorial stones stationed at important points, read the epitaphs of doom, and flee the luring valleys of poisonous influence and find refuge in Christ our Savior.

From Temonggoeng, we visited Djokykarta. Here also the interest was such in the meetings that the regular hall was abandoned and a larger one rented to accommodate the crowds seeking healing, deliverance from evil spirits, salvation, and the Holy Spirit. Praise God, our all-sufficient Savior could meet them all. We were happy to see these people rejoicing in the same blessed hope,

Our next meetings were in Koetoadjo. For two nights the Mission Hall was a scene of revival.

In Wonosoba, our next place to minister, we had a baptismal service, and I was privileged to immerse eleven Javanese in water.

We completed the itinerary by visiting Poerbalinga, Poerwakerta, Batabsarie, Cheribon,

Bandoeng and Batavia, the western section of Java and the capital of the Dutch East Indies. In each place we found open doors and open hearts to receive us. We were strangers and foreigners to every one in Java, but God miraculously opened every city for us, pouring out his blessings upon the meetings in a marked way.

Many have asked us what the food was like in Java. Well, we ate everything from delicious tropical fruit to duck eggs that had been buried some three months. Most of the food was so highly seasoned with red pepper that it made tears run out of our eyes while we ate it. Both of us had determined, as the Apostle Paul, to eat what was set before us, asking no questions for conscience sake.

In Java, there are three cities known to the natives as "Cities of Devils." In these three cities the doctors of black magic make their headquarters, and work throughout the entire Island. Millions of the poor natives of Java are ruled by the witch doctor. He is called in case of a family quarrel or in sickness. If you have an enemy that you want to die, pay him the price and your enemy will soon be in another world. Everyone highly respects him, and even worships him. We have ridden on buses through the country with a witch doctor on the same bus. He is the center of attraction; people meet the bus and shout to him.

We have seen him stop at a beautiful palatial home, take out his small attache case and knock on the back door, ready for business.

While visiting the village of Gambang Walla, the mayor of this hundred per cent Christian village gave his testimony. He was so enthusiastic that I asked our interpreter to translate it to me. The story is as follows.

Many years ago, when he was just a boy, he saw black magic and desired to have the power. Therefore, he went into the bush and fasted and prayed for ten days and nights, begging spirits to inhabit his body. At the end of this time a power gripped his body that threw him over and over on the ground, making him foam at the mouth like a mad dog. From this time, he had remarkable power and was recognized as a doctor of black art. Some of the things he says he did, and all the people in the village verified, are too weird for description.

Years later a Christian missionary woman appeared in the village and began teaching about Jesus, and healing the sick. The natives began flocking after her, and this made the witch doctor angry. He came to the meetings and sat and tried to throw his devilish influence over the missionary, so that she could not talk. He failed, although it did greatly disturb her.

He came a number of times until at last one

night in a fury he challenged the young lady, saying that if she had the most power he would leave the village, but if he had the most power she must leave. The missionary said, "Well, do something."

He walked to the front of the church before all the people and he lay down on the dirt floor perfectly motionless for a few moments. He became stiff; one could hardly see him breathe. Then he began to move; his feet, head, body, all on a level, gradually ascended. He floated knee high, waist high. This was the power of levitation being demonstrated.

"What can I do?" said the missionary girl. "I know I cannot float in the atmosphere." The natives were nearly hysterical seeing their master float. A thought came to the missionary that all she could do was to get him down. She reached and caught him in the chest, and shouted, "Come down, in Jesus' Name." Down he came, but started up again. Then she held him down.

The anointing of the Lord came upon her. The apostolic ministry of Mark 16:17 became hers. She began to rebuke the vile, unclean spirits, commanding them to loose their victim in the Name of of the Prince of Peace. The witch doctor went into convulsions, but she held him down. He choked and foamed at the mouth, his stomach moved on the inside as if something was coming out. The girl, trembling under the holy unction of God, bound those filthy demons, delivered him of them, and consigned them to the pit of hell. The missionary prayed that God would sweep and clean the temple and come in to dwell.

The witch doctor stood up. He felt himself all over, then looked at the people and then at the missionary. He said, "Something has happened; my power is gone; but I am happy in my heart." Praise God for a work that was done that night that has not ended yet.

Before the missionary would let the former witch doctor leave the church, she laid hands on him and prayed for him to receive the Holy Spirit. He received that night, and became a leading native preacher in that part of the country. He was elected the Honorable Mayor of Gambang Walla, the hundred per cent Christian village.

While in meetings in Bandoeng, Brother Carter was praying with a group of Christians to be filled with the Spirit. I was praying with some sinners to find Christ. A woman with an unclean spirit began to go through some strange movements in the meeting. Out she came to the front with her wild eyes and distorted face. We prayed for her and rebuked the foul spirit. With a hideous grin she said, "The devil is standing here by me, laughing at you." "Do you see him?" we asked. "Yes, he is laughing at you." In the name of Jesus Christ we reprimanded this power which bound her. She choked and went into a state of comatose.

We continued to pray until she opened her eyes and smiled. We shouted, "She is free." Her wild eyes were now as calm as a child's. With a tranquil look and a deep breath she said, "Peace, peace." I think she said it had been fifteen years since she had been bound by these unholy spirits. Hallelujah! Jesus is the same yesterday, today and forevermore.

The Javanese Sultan, whose name is Amangku Buwono, meaning, "He who has the world's axis on his knees," had given us permission to visit his palace. It was my first visit to any palace, and we were pleased to have this rare opportunity.

About eight-thirty in the morning, we took a taxi to the palace. In front is a large square with trees clipped and trained to the shape of monster unbrellas. The palace is one mile square, and is surrounded by a high white wall. It is a city inside the city of Djokjakarta.

The guard met us barefooted and wearing a sarong (skirt). We produced our pass and he unlocked the great iron gates and we walked inside. The gate closed behind us. The guard, now our guide, took us down a narrow way, up a flight of stairs, then down into a courtyard on the other side. Here we stopped. Pointing to a square block of wood with hacked places on it, our guide said, "This is the royal chop block. When a person used to lose the favor of His Majesty the Sultan, it was here he lost his head."

44

Straight across was the open-court throne where the Sultan holds his court. Sitting in pairs in intervals, cross-legged on the ground, were the royal guard holding their rifles across their knees. They were dressed in skirts and were bare-footed. Their main duty seemed to be smoking, laughing and talking. Just behind the throne we saw the Sultan's private orchestra made up of the queerest of instruments.

Passing by an open door leading into an apartment, we saw a number of girls who were crawling in at the door. We asked why they did not walk in. Our guide said they had to show submission to the Ratu, the head wife of the Sultan. They were her personal maids, coming into her presence, and they must not stand up in so doing.

As we were crossing a courtyard, someone whispered, "The Crown Prince." There moved a slow procession across the yard before us, coming to where we were standing. The Prince was a large, stout, awkward-looking man. He was wearing a sarong and sandals. Over him was a very large golden umbrella, held by two attendants, and behind him was a personal guard of some twenty or thirty men. The Prince nodded at us and spoke. We nodded back, and he passed on.

The guide took us next to see the Sultan's golden carriage of state. It was most magnificent. The interior was covered with purple velvet. Last of all we visited the Sultan's private temple, but the hideous gods were under repair, some getting a new coat of paint, others getting weak or broken parts fixed. As we left we noticed the priest following us about with his charger of incense burning. Our guide said we had defiled the palace, so incense had to be burned to purify it. We were sorry to defile the palace, but enjoyed the visit immensely.

Now I will relate our visit to a Javanese kampong or village. When we were in the city of Kediri we arose early one morning, and took a taxi for thirty miles, then a train for a further 150 miles, and a bus for about fifty more miles. This brought us to a very mountainous section of Java, where the cool breeze was refreshing after enduring the terrible heat of the cities. Here we stopped with a Dutch friend for the night.

The following morning we were up early, and after a hasty meal, we took a taxi for about eight miles. Here the road ended and the trail began. The lady missionary who had labored in this Javanese kampong for fifteen years was taken in a sedan chair, that is, a chair with bamboo poles fastened on each side. Four men carry the bamboo poles across their shoulders. Our suitcases were tied to these primitive people.

We trod over mountains, through valleys, around great boulders and by beautiful rice paddy fields.

As we came within a few miles of the village, the native pastor and some of the leading Christians met us, giving us a warm welcome to Gambang Walla. As we neared his home, which was a mile from the village, he constrained us to come in and have a cup of tea and a cake in his bamboo hut.

Soon we heard joyful singing and echoes of praise from enthusiastic hearts. Standing at the entrance to the village were little children, singing, "Hallelujah to the Lamb." Over the entrance was a flower-decked arch, supported by two large banana trees with fruit hanging from them. The Javanese said this was to signify our fruitful visit to their kampong.

As we walked by the beautiful little brown children with their faces shining with salvation's light, tears rushed to my eyes. Do missions pay? One glance at their smiling faces supplied the answer. Now we were in front of the bamboo house where we were to stay. All the villagers came out to look us over and to shake our hands and greet us in Javanese.

At last we were shown to our room, but had only been there a few minutes when we were asked to come out again, as the oldest person in the village, a blind woman, desired to pray for us. What a prayer that poor old peasant woman uttered with her head nearly touching the ground. She seemed to rock the heavens. Our interpreter could not explain it all for weeping, but said that she was praying for God to richly bless our visit to them.

We were with these people two days in meetings. The services were held in a bamboo tabernacle with an earth floor. For this occasion, the church was gorgeously decorated with beautiful flowers, ferns and green foliage. When ministering, our messages were interpreted from English into Dutch and then into Javanese, as the missionary to the Javanese did not understand English. This was a long and difficult way of presenting the gospel.

An extremely interesting episode was the wedding ceremony of a Javanese boy and girl. The young man, who was sitting with the men on one side of the church, came up to the front and sat in a flower-bedecked chair with his flaming Javanese skirt and barefooted. The young lady, in her beautiful colored sarong and with bare feet, also sat in a chair covered with flowers beside the groom. The missionary united them in marriage, and after they both had solemnly said "I will," she prayed over them, and then they arose and went to their respective seats, one on the one side of the church and the other on the opposite side.

At a testimony meeting different ones told how God had wonderfully saved and delivered them from sin. One had been a magic-dancer, performing by the power of the devil. Another had been a witch doctor, out of whom the lady missionary had cast demons. One feature marked them all, their great joy in serving God.

We walked about the village and saw the primitive little huts and beautiful rice fields. One evening supper was being prepared, and our interpreter took us to see the kitchen. It was a large room built behind the house. As we walked in, the room was full of smoke from the open fire in the center. Looking to one end, I saw the cook's bed with two or three children in it. Above us on a pole were about a dozen chickens, and another corner was the milk cow. In the middle of the room was the brick oven and our food cooking, while a pig and a dog walked about with eagerness looking for a morsel to eat. I learned in one visit that it is best never to see an Oriental kitchen, then one can eat the prepared mysteries with a little better appetite.

Our all too brief visit to Gambang Walla was at an end. We bade the villagers farewell and walked across the mountains until we reached the city life again. Our visit to Java was now drawing to a close. Over 3,000 miles of traveling in intense heat had been accomplished. God had blessed, with many souls being converted and baptized in the Holy Spirit.

In closing the story of Java, I will quote part of an article written by our Dutch brother, Mr. F. Van Abkoude, to the *Redemption Tidings*.

"We prayed God to send a messenger, and Brother Howard Carter came to Java with Brother Sumrall. We were glad to receive them in our home. They were God's messengers, and their message has brought a rich blessing to Java. I believe that each child of God has his own message. Brother Sumrall preached a message of repentance and salvation with blessed results. Brother Carter preached another message, and God confirmed his words with 'signs following.' At first I was surprised to see believers filled and baptized with the Holy Ghost in a few minutes. It was a wonderful ministry and full of blessing. Souls have been saved, healed and baptized with the Holy Spirit. The result of their ministry will be seen in eternity."

Chapter 5

SINGAPORE AND HONG KONG

SINGAPORE, what a profusion of pictures its name produces! Everyone has heard of this great island city, situated as Asia's cornerstone, lying just off her southeastern coast. Travelers know her as a glamorous cosmopolitan city, almost sitting astride the equator, where every race, color and blood meet together. Mariners know her as the "crossroads of the world," in whose port you find every flag under heaven flying. It is also their chief coaling station on the route between Europe and the Far East.

To the merchantmen of the world, Singapore is the seventh port in importance, with harbor and docks second to none, and a rich market with cheap Asiatic labor.

Singapore to the statesmen of the world is Britain's impregnable naval base of awesome proportions, which stands out as a peace monument to those seeking peace, but a hideous monster, lying in wait to strike, to those who make aggression their sole ambition.

Singapore, to the missionary, is another great

city with every cult and religion of the world there, as a challenge to her supreme place in the hearts of all mankind.

On the morning of our arrival from Java, to the first of Britain's Oriental islet-twins, the city lay bathed in golden sunshine, not to speak of its great sweltering heat, as it lies only seventy-eight miles from the imaginary line called the equator.

The ultra-beautiful islet-dotted harbor had every kind of boat from the modern floating palace to thousands of Chinese junks with their sails patched with multi-colored rags.

As soon as the *Marella* opened her gang-way, up the plank came the Oriental money-changers. They hastily covered the ship, approaching every passenger, and, holding out a handful of coins, offered a good exchange price. We believed their story and bought a few Singapore dollars, but when we found the current rate of exchange, we understood why Jesus chased them out of the Temple, saying they made the House of Worship a den of thieves!

We made contact here with Mr. Cecil Jackson, an American missionary. Brother Jackson was a stranger to us, but only for a moment. His every thought seemed to be for our pleasure and comfort while with him.

In the evening we spoke at his mission hall. It was filled to capacity with eager hearts to hear God's Word.

After a few inspiring songs, Brother Carter spoke, administering spiritual bread and wine to the Christians present. Afterward I gave a short evangelistic talk and threw out the Gospel net. Sixteen honest-hearted folk went into the prayer room to come forth new creatures in Christ Jesus. Among them was a ship captain, his wife and one of his crew, who did not even know how to pray, but repeated a prayer after the pastor, confessing his sins. He left the prayer room happy in his newly-found Savior. The daughter of a former rubber multi-millionaire also came with tears and confession to God.

The next morning Mr. Jackson took us for a tour in his car about the island city, which is only twenty-eight miles in length and fourteen miles in width, and also over on the Malay Peninsula to Johore. He told us an inspiring story about his missionary work among the Sakai aborigines, about two weeks' journey up the peninsula. It was inspiring to hear of their eagerness to receive the glorious story of a Savior.

In the evening we had another great meeting. The Lord so graciously blessed our efforts that our friends urged us to stay longer, and take our campaign to the large Victoria Hall; but engagements in China prevented this.

With a promise to return as soon as God permitted, we bade our new friends and their beautiful island-home farewell, and boarded an ocean liner and steamed north.

As the steel prow of our giant ship cut vigorously through the deep blue waters, where for centuries pirate ships had lurked, seeking an innocent passer-by, we looked back and said, "Lord, bless Singapore, and give it a real Pentecostal Revival!"

I was walking along the promenade deck of the S.S. *Terukuna Maru* early one morning breathing my devotion to God. We were traveling through the South China Sea, and in the distance I could dimly see the small tropical islands surrounding the Crown Colony of Hong Kong, the other of Britain's islet twins of the East.

As I ascended the top-deck of the ship, to my amazement I saw a man bowing and saluting the rising sun, praying in his native tongue. "A sun worshipper!" I exclaimed. After continuing his homage several minutes, he turned and walked away. How my heart rejoiced more than ever, in that I was not worshipping the sun, but the Creator of the universe, who made our sun and thousands more just as brilliant to travel in their orbits and shine a praise to their Maker.

I stood in the prow and watched our approach to Hong Kong, the great crescent-shaped port. Since a small boy, I had read and heard the weird and wonderful stories of Asia's Middle Kingdom; now my heart beat faster as we were only a few minutes away from it. We rounded a small island, which has a great white lighthouse towering on its peak, and came into full view of the famous and impressive Victoria Peak, lifting its proud and imposing shoulders 1,825 feet above the horizon. China at last!

Soon we were in the harbor. On one side of us was the magnificent sky-line of modern buildings, on the other was Kowloon, the residential section. As soon as we were sighted, sampans came scuttling from everywhere, and swarmed about the steamer. The Chinese beggars with their high shrill voices chattered loudly, with their long thin arms extended upward and gesticulating wildly, desiring a coin to be thrown to them. Others, more professional, had long bamboo poles with a little sack tied on the end and pushed them up the side of the vessel to receive their contribution from the foreigners.

Soon we had pulled alongside the dock at Kowloon, and, as Hong Kong is an open port, the pleasure of travel was not marred by an official molestation seeking to unpack our suitcases for us.

As we looked down on to the wharf, new things for our eyes could be seen. The coolie with his big umbrella hat and naked down to his waist. The large muscular Sikh (Indian policeman from British India) coming on board with his long hair rolled around his head. His job was to watch for thieves. As we were standing by the rail, we saw a Sikh pulling a poor Chinaman up the dock, kicking him as he went. He had evidently broken the law. All the foreigners standing around were dressed in white, it being too hot to dress otherwise.

To our surprise, we were met at the docks by two of Brother Carter's former Bible school students, who are now missionaries to Yunnan province. At present they were obliged to evacuate their station and take refuge in Hong Kong, as the Communists were raging in their section, leaving devastation and death in their path.

Later, we were introduced to a number of missionaries who had gathered in Hong Kong for the special meetings. We met others whom we had known in the homeland, and joyfully renewed old-time friendships. What a welcome! Everyone seemed so happy, looking forward to a great refreshing in the Lord during the revival meetings. The missionaries stated that we were the only ministers who had ever come out from the homeland to visit them, for the sole purpose of conducting special campaigns.

A large flat had been secured for all visitors who had come to stay for the special meetings. Soon we settled down in our temporary home, and commenced to look around us. The term "noisy

China" is very fitting. In the streets men were uttering some weird and uncanny shrieks, but we were assured that they were only selling their wares. The clatter of hundreds of wooden shoes resounding on the pavement was nearly unbearable. Then the people in the flat opposite turned on the radio or gramophone—all in Chinese! In climbing the three flights of stairs to our flat, we had seen the hideous "God of the Door" pasted on the front door. The superstitious Chinese believe it gives protection. Some incense sticks were burning by it in a container.

Our ten days in Hong Kong were very busy. We enjoyed everything, from the wonderful revival meetings to the trip to Victoria Peak by electric-cable car, where a view almost unparalleled met our eyes. While in Hong Kong, there were three meetings each day in the church, plus the interesting round-the-table discussions after each meal with the missionaries.

The first service of each day was at nine a.m. This was for missionaries and those who understood English. Brother Carter gave Bible studies on deeper spiritual life, which proved to be immensely appreciated. One could hear it being said after these talks, "We have never heard it in this fashion before!" It proved the strength of Christian fellowship, as missionaries from various countries and from different religious organizations came to these meetings, and received a rich infilling of the Holy Spirit.

Next came the eleven a.m. service. This was a general meeting, the message being interpreted into Chinese. Each morning the large hall was nearly filled, mostly with Christians.

The song service was really inspiring as Mrs. Williamson led it most enthusiastically with her tambourine. The Chinese, in general, dearly love drums, tambourines, cymbals, etc. The more noise the better! As the Chinese try to fit their intonations to our sacred hymns, it leaves you minus the tune, but that does not cause any bother in China!

A number of Christians received a definite baptism of the Spirit in the waiting meetings. Mr. Williamson brought his entire young men's Bible school down from Canton to be in these meetings. Every one of the young men received the Holy Spirit while in Hong Kong.

A tidal wave of blessing seemed to pass through the evening evangelistic services. The large tabernacle would be packed out, with people standing in every available space, and children sitting around the platform. The atmosphere was suffocating; almost everyone used a fan. This was a sight to behold. The Lord moved upon the unconverted in a striking way. Conviction swept the audience each night, and a harvest of souls were laid at the Master's feet. There were numbers of young people who came to Christ with tears. Two young Chinese men who had heard the Gospel in London, England, now accepted the truth back home in Hong Kong.

There were always many sick people needing prayer. So we prayed for them after each meeting. Some wonderful healings took place. The Chinese do things we would never dream of doing. On several occasions I would see the same one to be prayed for again and again. I would ask, "But did not the Lord heal you?" "Yes, yes, I am healed, but pray for me again, then after you are gone, if I get sick, this prayer will heal me." Blessing in store for future trouble is Oriental wisdom?!

On the last night of our special meetings in Hong Kong there was an impressive baptismal service. A number of the Chinese men and women dressed in their white gowns entered with their pastor into the baptistery, to make a public confession of Christ by following him into the watery grave, to come forth and walk in newness of life as an example to this sinful world.

As I have not mentioned the care of the Lord in providing for our needs since leaving Australia, I feel that I should give a few of thc incidents here.

Through Australia and Java our needs were quickly met. When thin clothing was needed in Java, about three or four suits were given to both of us. When tickets were needed, the money was at hand. The Lord has a variety of ways in dealing with His children. Sometimes He waits until the last moment, then comes to the rescue to prove His faithfulness to us.

From Hong Kong, we desired to travel some 3,500 miles on a tour to the borders of Burma and Tibet. This would take many weeks, and a considerable amount of money, with no prospects of finance from the natives en route. In our mail from America only a few dollars had been received from friends who had felt led to assist us. On the night before we were to buy our tickets on the following day, the native church gave us a love offering. We only expected a few dollars in Hong Kong, but no, one Chinese lady felt she must give us one hundred and sixty dollars. Also a number of Chinese Christians brought canned foods for us to take inland. These nearly saved our lives later. Every one was greatly surprised about the offering. The missionary pastor said the congregation did not usually pay the current expenses of their church. Our God saw the long arduous journey and our needs. Praise the Lord, He supplied! There is a saying that in China when you take up an offering your congregation gets up and leaves. We did not find this so. Even the primitive tribal people (Lisu) near Burma gave a liberal offering of twenty dollars. How it does make you appreciate people who love the Gospel sufficiently to support it.

When we arrived at the nearest missionary station to Tibet, we found our funds rather low, and it was a very bad place to get low. The trip inland was costing more than we anticipated, but thank the Lord, at our very next stop, most unexpectedly, a missionary who knew nothing of our needs, felt led of God to give us a sum of money. This took us on a few more days when the Lord moved in another remarkable way, and we arrived back in the capital with a few dollars in hand.

On another occasion our tickets which we had bought for a return journey were only valid for sixty days, and we had been gone nearly ninety days. We felt we could not afford to lose these return tickets as they were very expensive. We prayed about it and asked God to make the tickets valid in some way. After prayer, the resident missionary, Mr. Wood, sent them to an official of the French Railroad for us. The members of the board of directors, after consultation, agreed unanimously to extend our tickets to ninety days, thereby making them valid. Our hearts were made to rejoice that our God can even change French Railroad laws, and give a distressed child of His favor with a board of directors.

A lady was recounting to me how the Lord had told her to send me twenty-five dollars. We were crossing Russia at this time. But the lady wanted to give this money to another cause, so she told the Lord she did not know where I was, and the Lord told her how to send it, but yet she declined to do so. For some days she had a battle in her soul, until at last she sent the check. A great story could be told of how that money was made a blessing. God saw to it that it did not arrive a day late.

One other incident I would like to relate. When we were in London on our last visit, I was greatly looking forward to the time of crossing the Atlantic and seeing my loved ones and friends again, but had no money for the fare. This matter was taken before the Lord daily. Then the Lord moved some Christian woman's heart and she sent Brother Carter and myself £50, Also someone felt led to send me a new pair of shoes, which fitted perfectly, and I now could discard my ill-fitting Chinese pair. Praise God, He feedeth the ravens and clotheth the lilies.

Chapter 6

BACKWARD YUNNAN

CHINA has a place named Yunnan, that very few people know anything about, not even the Chinese themselves.

For one thing, it is a very difficult place to reach. Then the people are more ignorant and backward than in any other section of China. Until the French Government built their remarkable railroad to its capital, few white people other than missionaries had seen it.

In olden times, when the Chinese Emperors in Peiping desired to banish a dangerous character, they would send him far over the mountains to southwest China, now known as Yunnan Province. For many, many years they dumped desperadoes there, and from them sprang the Yunnanese of today. They are a poor, degenerate, half-caste (Chinese and tribal people) ignorant folk, who live in a world to themselves, under conditions such as existed a thousand years ago. They plow with a wooden plow and ox. They grind grain by rubbing stones together, and live in their adobe houses (clay brick).

Mr. Carter, Mr. Boyd, an English missionary, our interpreter and I went to this far off the beaten track Yunnan to visit the missionaries. Leaving Hong Kong, we took the S.S. *Canton,* a small combination steamer, across the stormy gulf of Tonking to French Indo-China. Eventually the ship plowed into the muddy bay of Haiphong and docked at the wharf. The heat was almost unbearable in this sultry tropical city. We disembarked and passed our baggage through the customs, and as our train did not leave until the following morning, we went for a walk about the city. Haiphong being in the tropics, its parks and palm-shaped boulevards were exceedingly beautiful. We noticed nearly every native woman had shining black teeth.We were told that the women think black teeth very pretty, so they enamel them black.

The following morning our little mountain train pulled out of Haiphong, puffing and blowing with a chug, chug, chug. We were off for a three day run through Tonking Indo-China and Yunnan.

All day we rode through some of the most exquisite tropical scenery. As there is no restaurant car on the train, and no stopping for food, the traveler is obliged to carry his own along with him. This we did and enjoyed it. We had a little oil stove to heat water for tea, and opened tins of food.

In the evening we arrived at Laogay, the border town separating French Indo-China from China. As the railroad is dangerous, and the mountains very high, the train does not travel at night. Passengers, train and all just stop over until the next morning. We had to find a room and food in a local hotel. We wound our way up an alley following a porter, then ascended a narrow, dirty staircase, walked down a long dark hall, into a small dingy room with two beds. As the corpulent landlord left the room, he warned us against rats, roaches, bugs and a few other of "China's millions" which we were better acquainted with by the next morning.

At six a.m. we were off again. In five minutes after departing we had entered a tunnel, and for the rest of the day we went in and out of tunnels. I agreed before evening that this railway was one of the most remarkable feats of engineering in the world. There was so much dynamiting in blasting these tunnels through the mountains that it is said that there is a dead Chinaman for each sleeper on the track. The curves were so sharp that you could look out of the window and see the rear coaches entering the tunnel you had just come out of. On emerging from each tunnel the carriage was full of smoke, cinders, etc., as there were no screens on the windows and it was too hot to have them closed. I have been nearly a thousand miles by airplane on one journey, and experienced some tough storms at sea, and even had a ride on a camel, but have never been travel-sick until this little French train swung us through about 300 tunnels towering in the peaks of China's mountains. There were some rare sights such as a very small bridge suspended over a chasm between two tunnels, on a curve, where you could watch the other carriages go over it. There were two or three exquisite cascades, nearly covered with luxuriant growth, gliding over a precipice. Also some beautiful lakes situated at the top of the mountains.

In the evening we arrived in Amicheo, where Miss Agar, one of our American missionaries, has a station. We had a meeting in her mission hall. In the song service there were about thirty voices singing, and I think there must have been about twenty-nine different tunes sung at once. Mr. Boyd was leading the singing. A wooden partition was built down the center of the church, as the men do not want to see the despised women as they are worshipping.

Mr. Carter gave the first message, with Mr. Boyd interpreting. As he spoke, the Chinese listened intently for a moment or two, and then turned to a neighbor and discussed the speaker in loud tones. As Brother Carter was making clear a very interesting point, three of his best listeners got up and walked out. He brought his sermon to a close.

This is typical of the east. Following this I spoke for a few minutes, then asked for decisions for Christ. A few responded.

The next morning at six o'clock the sturdy little train blew its whistle and we continued our trip inland. We passed some rather large towns during the day, each had a high clay wall around it. A few missionaries got aboard the train *en route* for the special meetings to be held in the capital.

About five o'clock in the afternoon we arrived in Yunnanfu, the capital city of the great province of Yunnan, southwest China.

What a shout arose as we pulled into the station! It was a great meeting together, everyone telling how long it had been since seeing one another; some stating how many months it had been since they had even seen a white face. Quite a number of missionaries from all over the province had gathered for the special conference and for a time of fellowship.

From the station we rode in a rickshaw through the huge gates of the walled city, with guards standing overhead, guns in hand. We gazed in wonder at the quaint hieroglyphics and carvings on the magnificent architecture of this old city.

One of the first things a westerner notices is the small bound feet of the Chinese women, moving about the streets. The size of the feet varies from three, four and five inches in length. It gives a strangeness to the whole body. The deformity causes the legs not to mature.

As the rickshaws bumped along on the worn rough cobble stones of the narrow streets, the people gazed and stared at us. They were as interesting to us as we were to them, so we returned the compliment.

Our initiation into cruel China came in our first ten minutes in the capital. Our rickshaws passed a group of men who were stoning a man to death. He groaned and screamed as large stones tore his body. The men and women looked on and laughed, and someone commented that he was a thief.

Once inside the gates of the mission house, however, we immediately felt the warmth of Christian love and fellowship with our missionaries.

The next day the Chinese language teacher came over and gave us a name, as our English names did not translate well. I cannot pronounce Mr. Carter's new name, but its meaning was "adding excellent virtue." The teacher named me "Song-yin-Leo."

For two weeks we sat in conference with the missionaries. The morning meetings were devotional, all the English speaking people of the city being invited. Everyone present enjoyed these times of blessing as the Word of God was expounded, or someone related a thrilling experience on their mission station.

The afternoons were devoted to the business sessions. The Lord graciously blessed each session with His presence. His guiding hand was ever felt in a remarkable way, and with His love predominating, difficulties were vanquished. In the evening the meetings were in the mission hall for the Chinese.

Experiences that linger a lifetime were acquired here. To gather the crowd, the missionary would blow his trumpet in front of the large hall, and in five or ten minutes it would be filled. After a hymn and prayer, the speaker began. Everyone listened intently for some five minutes, then, in a grand stampede, two thirds of them would get up and walk out, leaving you stammering in the pulpit. Mr. Carter and I developed some drastic gymnastics to keep the people entertained while speaking, but even this failed sometimes, and the concluding remarks of our sermon were addressed to the empty benches.

On Sunday morning I was asked to preach to the men only. As I repeated my text, a young man came in with his teapot and served tea to all. During my talk, the men sipped Chinese tea and then listened awhile. After the message I gave an invitation for sinners to come to Christ. The most intelligent looking man in the audience raised his hand and said, "I accept Christ." Then a few more followed. We took these to one side and prayed with them. I was very jubilant over the new converts, until, when the prayer was over, right in the church, our fine-looking gentleman said, "Which of you Americans want to buy some asbestos? I am a salesman." Well, we lost our "convert," for he was only practicing some Oriental diplomacy!

While In Yunnanfu, Mr. Colley and Miss Cummings, from England, were united in marriage by Brother Carter. I stood with the groom as his best man. The mission station was astir with excitement on this day. The sitting room was decorated beautifully for the occasion. Nearly all the missionaries of the city were present. The service was simple and short, after which the party went to the consulate where civil confirmation of the marriage was given. For the honeymoon this brave couple set out with us for the wilds of the Tibetan border, where danger and death lurk in every shadow. Living a few days away from the nearest white person, may God bless them as they labor for His Kingdom.

During our stay in Yunnanfu the missionaries asked us if we would like to visit a slave market. Not knowing that such things still existed in our enlightened age, we desired to see it.

The missionary lady cooked a basket of little cakes for the slave girls, and we crossed the city to the market. We found the slave girls in a vile women's prison. The most sinful and degraded women in the land were to be the first tutors in shaping the career of these innocent little girls.

As the guard opened the doors and consented to let us in, we noticed an information board on the wall, and tacked on it were the pictures of the little girls who were on the block for sale that day. We were shown their living quarters. It consisted of a one-room apartment, dirty and filthy, and infested with rats, lice, fleas, roaches and bugs. Across the courtyard was a wooden door with a hole some ten or twelve inches square in it. Through this aperture a few eyes could be seen attempting to look at us. Someone whispered, "The slave girls!"

The door was opened, and out from their prison filed twenty-four little creatures. I gazed in amazement. We were beholding a scene that nearly made one doubt the verity of our eyesight. Coming straggling along and looking wonderingly at us, they hardly looked human. They were ragged and dirty. Their hair had not been cut but broken off at various lengths. Their faces had been marred by abuse, and scars were on their bodies received from inmates and the slave master. Was this the result of 3,000 years' civilization without the Living God?

The lady missionary took the girls to a corner, lined them in a row, and began to teach them a chorus.

Jesus loves the little children,
All the children are His care,
Red and yellow, black and white,
They are precious in His sight,
Jesus loves the little children everywhere.

Yes, Jesus loves you dear little castaways; your awful plight is His care, was my heart's sigh.

As the little girls stood mumbling these strange words, we sought to learn their price. The slavekeeper said one of them could be bought for about three shillings, others up to thirty shillings. A native could buy one cheaper. The disfigured, emaciated, imbeciles could be bought for a few pence. Once bought they are the slave of the buyer as long as life is in the body. After prayer, the lady missionary opened her basket and gave these children the cakes. It was heartbreaking to see them choking down the cakes. They had not had anything so nice for a long time, and in all probability the missionary would have to bring the next cakes they would receive. We now turned to go away and the girls were herded back into their prison. After returning to my room, I prayed God to help them. It rejoiced my heart to read of Christian ladies in England who were stirred by my article in *Redemption Tidings* and impressed of the Lord to buy some of these girls and have them reared to be Gospel workers. Some very lovely characters have been found in this manner and today have a great message, that once they were a slave but Jesus had set them free.

Let us go across the city to the rescue home which is run by some German Christian women. When missionaries buy slave girls, they place them here for training. We arrived as the girls were eating supper. As we walked into the dining room the little girls had a bowl of rice in one hand and chopsticks poised in the other; and the rice was fast disappearing! These little girls had clean white aprons on; their faces and hands were clean; hair had been neatly trimmed, and all dirty sores had been attended to. The matron showed us some beautiful needlework they were doing to help support themselves. Everything in the rescue orphanage had an air of happiness about it.

This was not the end of our acquaintance with the slave girls. While we were traveling to the Tibetan border, nearly every horse inn had a slave to do the dirtiest work, and in recompence received what little rice is left over, or what she could steal, when no one was looking.

One night the furniture in our apartment consisted of one large red coffin, but caskets can do no harm, so we laid our clothes on it and went to sleep. The next night our apartment had a nest of rags in the corner, and when we investigated them a slave girl was found almost dead. Mr. Carter had our interpreter to talk to the innkeeper about it. "Bah, she is just an old slave who has worked all that she is able. Let her lay there and die," and off he went to leave her to die the death of a slave girl.

One of our missionaries went into a Chinese home and saw a slave girl grinding grain at the ancient stone mill, which is an animal's work. The missionary scolded the Chinese for such cruelty. They only replied that they had a donkey, but the donkey died, and not having money to purchase another, they just hitched up the slave girl to the mill. The missionary looked at the slave girl, and she had gone blind from going around in one circle all day in the intense heat.

Another friend said she was walking by a house when a slave girl ran to the open gate and fell dead near her. She looked around and there stood the dead girl's mistress with a stick in hand. "Why did you kill her," she asked. "She would not obey me," said the Chinese woman, "and it does not matter if she is dead." With an air of satisfaction she turned and walked away from the scarred dead body. Surely what the world needs is Jesus; just one glimpse of His LOVE and compassion.

Chapter 7

TO THE TIBETAN BORDER ON MULE BACK

" LOOK, Brother Carter, our private bodyguard! See their shining muskets, those blue trousers and black caps. Doesn't that produce an air of importance?"

We had bidden the missionaries adieu, walked through the city and out of the west gate of Yunnanfu, followed by our mule caravan of some fifteen animals, heading for the borders of Tibet and Burma.

Here the last of modern civilization ended, and we took the "lightning express" which averaged the speed of ten li per hour (about three English miles). This was to last for nine long weeks. My "coach" had no electric light, and in fact had no roof to keep us dry. It did have long ears, a long face, a profound look and a stubborn will. Yes, you have guessed its name. The saddle I rode on was made of hardwood in a V shape and slipped down on the mule's back. Over the wooden saddle you tie your bedding (as there are no beds for hire in this section), then ride on top, in a kind of dromedary style.

The most dangerous and fatiguing part of the whole tour had begun. The missionaries said it was the "wet season," and no one travels for a long distance, unless compelled, for when it rains in China it pours. Horse roads are gone and even villages are washed away in a very short time.

The British and American consuls said it was very dangerous to take this journey, as a few straggling Communists and robber bands would be on the route. These would be glad of the privilege of capturing us for ransom, or severing our heads from our shoulders, as they had done John and Betty Stam a few weeks before. Mr. Bosshardt, a C.I.M. missionary, was being held for ransom somewhere in that section at this time. He was set free after eighteen months' captivity.

We felt it the Lord's will to visit the far inland mission stations, therefore we decided to undertake the venture. The Consulate sent a guard of soldiers with us for protection.

Outside the city, we got astride our animals and soon lost sight of Yunnanfu. Our first day we followed a narrow path made of rocks. It had just rained and they were very slippery. This made it difficult for the animals to walk. The mule I rode, which I named "Henry," had a bad temper. He would walk a few steps and then kick furiously. I presumed that he did not desire his passenger.

We did not get far the first day. About five p.m. we sheltered in a muddy village named Pi-chi-kuan. As there are no hotels, we stayed in the horse inn, our apartment being the loft with pigs, goats, cows and horses just underneath prancing and pushing all night.

The next morning the sun was shining beautifully, so our caravan, which consisted of Mr. Carter, Mr. Boyd, Mr. Colley and myself, with a Chinese cook and the muleteers who hired the animals to us, made a good start and did the day's stage in record time.

Our first mission station visited was that of Miss Wright. She is an American girl, and was living upstairs over a filthy stable. She was the only foreigner in the entire city. In the evening she called her band of Christians together and we had a short meeting.

As the days passed, the scenery became more and more beautiful. We journeyed through deep rock ravines, over narrow ledges at dazzling heights, with a roaring river below us. At times two or three ranges of mountains peeped up behind each other. No wonder Yunnan is called the Switzerland of China.

One feature of our inland tour that is precious to our hearts was the fellowship with missionaries of different countries, Germany, Holland, Scandinavia, Australia and others. The barriers of denominationalism and nationalism were torn down completely. Everyone offered us hospitality in their compound and ministry in their churches.

At Chien-chuen we stopped for a couple of days at the station of Mr. C. Francis, a Welch brother. Here the Chinese prepared us a feast to which they invited the landlord. There were seventeen or eighteen courses served, the first being melon seed, and the last being an extra bowl of rice with plenty of fat pork.

In the meeting at the mission hall one evening there was a man who wanted the people to leave the church, so he jumped up and said, "The foreigners are crazy," and walked out. Only a few followed him. He then came to the door and shouted that a bad storm was coming up. All the Chinese jumped up and ran out into the street, but found the stars shining. Most of them left the church, so we closed the meeting. The fickleness of a Chinese congregation is well-known. When friends asked us what it was like preaching to the natives far inland, I told them I thought our sermons had three effects on the congregation. They were moving, soothing and satisfying. Moving, because as we began to speak the people moved out of the door. Soothing, because they who stayed usually went to sleep. Satisfying, because we never saw the same congregation twice!

We had a few thrilling episodes to add interest to this lonely mule ride over vast plains and high mountains. One day we found Mr. Carter upside down in a cactus hedge, after slipping with hands and feet around his mule's neck, saying, "Whoa! Whoa!" but that Chinese mule did not understand English. Mr. Carter soon landed on the ground.

One day, as I saw a hole of water, I asked Henry if he wanted a drink, and pulled him over to it. As he took a drink, I suppose the wooden saddle irritated that awful running sore on his back, for his heels took a forty-five degree angle and I found myself neck deep in the mud hole. Of course I went in head first!

At another time, we were crossing a long muddy stretch of road; the other mules had passed through it. My mule got half way, raised his nose and sniffed a few times, lay down and rolled over. As soon as I walked out, with mud nearly to my knees he got up and followed me. Such escapades as these delighted the Chinese; they would roar with laughter.

One morning, our caravan walked slowly out of a village where we had spent the night, with five or six other caravans. I was seated on Henry reading. It must have been an hour later that I looked up, and to my amazement could not see a white person. I looked at the Chinese, but did not recognize any of them, they only laughed at me. We rode on for another hour, and I did not see anyone I knew. I came to the conclusion that I was on the wrong road and lost. One thousand five hundred miles from Hong Kong and lost! I could not speak a word of Chinese and did not have a penny of money on my person. Now Henry sensed we were lost. He threw his head high in the air and began to bellow. It was awful! Henry's regular gait was three miles per hour, but now he broke loose and ran. He must have been making eight or ten miles per hour, and I was going up and down on his back, saying, "Whoa, Henry, whoa." Soon we were not with any caravan. Coming to the back of a mountain, I prayed, "Lord, please show me the way to go," then took the left hand around the mountain. We went for fifteen minutes when a man met us and began to jabber in that strange Chinese tongue. I shook my head, but he grabbed Henry by the head, turned him around and kicked him a few times. I yelled "Don't," but Henry was gone at a gallop. We went around the right side of the mountain, and an hour later found our caravan which had stopped to eat dinner, and was wondering where I had gone.

My diary for July 31st records that we walked across a swinging bridge suspended with chains and a rushing river beneath us. At noon, Mr. Colley and I went for a swim in the Yangtze-kiang river. The towering mountains covered with luxuriant growth with the beautiful river raging beneath is a worthy sight to see. Tonight we are sleeping in a barn nearly full of opium poppies. They are the seed for next year's sowing.

Some think opium is not grown in China any more, but she reaps a colossal harvest of it each year. Opium is sold at nearly every store in some inland cities. We saw many people smoking this dreadful poppy juice which benumbs the faculties and saps all the vitality from the system. We have seen Chinese from a five-year-old boy to an old man lying down smoking.

Twenty-nine days after we had left Yunnanfu, we arrived in Chu-Tien where Mr. and Mrs. Colley were to labor. The people here are mostly Tibetans. This section was Tibet until the Chinese pushed them farther into the mountains.

From Chu Tien we turned southwest and climbed the lofty, rugged, wild mountains to 13,500 feet, and after two days travelling we arrived in Wei Shi. Here we spoke to the tribal people. The Lisu in Wei Shi were from the mountains near Burma. They are a rough primitive people with coarse features and home-spun clothes. An astonishing work has been done among them. Hundreds have been converted to Christianity. When the Lisu come to church, they start greeting you a great distance away, and as they come nearer and nearer, you hear them in their own tongue say

81

"Peace to you" over and over again. The last night we were there, numbers of them slept on the mission floor in order to give us a farewell early the following morning.

Traveling four days south from Wei Shu over wild mountains we came to Lan P'ing. Here we stood on a high peak and viewed beautiful tropical Burma. As the rain had fallen and the roads were gone, we had to have a special guide to direct us. Two or three times, very dangerous streams had to be forded. Twice we had to repair the road before the mules could pass. The narrow road had caved into a deep ravine in one place, so we had to cut the mountain away, making a path for the animals.

One night in this section, we had great difficulty in finding a place to stay. When we did, the landlady came in stamping her little four-inch feet and telling us to leave, but as the forest outside was full of wild animals, we just told her that we were spending the night there. The next morning, when she was well paid for the use of her barn, she became very amiable to the foreigners.

Mr. Fisher, the missionary stationed at Lan P'ing, met us a half-day's journey away with a basket of English food. I nearly weep yet to think about it. We felt nearly starved, as we had eaten Chinese food, when we could get it, until we had become weak. When he opened his basket and said grace, we sat down on the ground and ate ravenously. We shall never forget this act of kindness.

Our experiences were many and varied in this part of the country. To throw more light on our living conditions, I will relate a few incidents.

Our caravan moved slowly out of the small Chinese village in a heavy rainstorm. We were seated on our mules with large oil capes around us. We came to a place where our animals could not pass, therefore we had to climb an embankment to go around. Henry got half-way up and fell into a ditch. Off his back I came. After some time I managed to pull him out, and we two muddy creatures moved along to catch up with the caravan.

At noon we came to a very small village and stopped at the "cafe" for lunch. As we walked into the room, it was so full of smoke that we could hardly see. The table had a cloth on it made of layers of spilled food, soot, grease, etc. We looked to one side and saw the cook who was naked all but for a loincloth, standing by his brick furnace that had no chimney. He had a large iron pot on the furnace where everything was cooked. On one side of us was a dog, and on the other a pig; the floor was earthen. We noticed that the cook had a rag tied around his head. This was used for cleaning out the cooking pot. The dog got in his way, so he hit him with the rag and threw it back across his shoulder. Being near the furnace, he became warm, so he took the rag and wiped the perspiration off his body. As our dinner was cooking, he walked over to the door for some fresh air and used this same cloth for a handkerchief. When the food was ready to eat, he reached for some bowls, wiped them out with the same rag and put our food in them. Yes, we ate it. Great hunger can cause a man to swing to vast extremes.

We found that the Chinese would take things that belonged to us. One morning I found my best fountain pen gone. Another morning all our tin plates were missing. We were obliged to carry everything we needed while traveling here. Now breakfast could not be served until they were found. We asked the landlady about them, but she said, "I am sure no one in this village would steal."

We had been told that the only way to get things returned was to appear angry and demand them. We threatened not to pay for our lodgings if they were not found, but this had no effect. One of the party proposed sending for the magistrate of the village if they were not returned. This had effect. The landlady went to a filthy barrel of pig food, rolled up her sleeves and reached to the bottom, and up came our tin plates. You can imagine how nice it was to eat out of them after this experience.

Our caravan wound its way down the steep mountainside in single file. In the distant valley we could see a village clearly outlined by the rays of the setting sun, the clay wall with its Oriental tower over the gate for the watchman, predominating. The pagoda, usually painted white resembling a lighthouse, can be seen on a small hill-slope nearby. The Chinese believe the devils would destroy their city and bring some terrible plague upon them were it not for the protection of the pagoda.

Arriving at the huge gates, we alight from our animals while the people gaze intently at the foreigners, some laughing at us. Our interpreter says he hears remarks like this, "My, but the foreign devil has big feet," "What a long nose, and poor man he is blind." They think this because of our blue eyes, as all Chinese have black eyes.

We walked through the narrow street leading our mules, pushing stubborn pigs and dogs to one side and crying, "yield the way" to the slow moving Chinese. After stopping at three or four horse inns, we found one suitable for ourselves and animals. One does not ask if he may stay, but finds one sufficiently large and clean enough and stops. We led our animals through the large double doors into the first courtyard where their loads were removed. We went upstairs to our room, a large loft, removed the debris from the floor, and called for our bedding, cots and food box to be brought up. Below us during the night will be the horses, mules, goats, sheep, chickens or whatever the inn-keeper might own.

After prayer and thanksgiving for journeying mercies we are ready to set up housekeeping for a few hours. A few irritating bites made us aware of the presence of other occupants! Looking about the room, we noticed the homeshrine, its size and the number of idols being according to the wealth of the family. Some grain or flowers or food is placed on these altars, with incense burning to the gods. Over in the corner might be seen a long rough hewn box made of timber six inches thick. That will be grandmother's or grandfather's coffin awaiting the day when death shall lay them low. The Chinese take a pride in having their coffin prepared long before death is expected.

Everything being prepared for sleeping, we glance through a small aperture down on to the street. The little shops are selling their wares, the keeper always arguing at least five minutes about the price. Yonder is a group of little girls playing hop-scotch, just as in England or America, only strapped to their little backs is the baby of the family, getting a terrific jolt at every jump of its big sister.

A look into the next room reveals from one to eight people lying on a wooden bed, with their opium pipes. It takes the opium smoker from one to three hours to become stupefied according to how long he has been an addict. The forlorn-looking undeveloped little creature, ragged and filthy from doing the dirtiest work around the inn, is the slave girl of the home. Someone now says, "Come to food, pastors." And we all gather around the little table and receive a bowl of rice and chopsticks. The sudden report of a rifle is only the watchman giving the hour of the day.

It being now time to retire, the many curious onlookers are asked to depart. Sometimes they leave and sometimes not. Twice we were compelled to retire while the visitors looked on interestedly.

There were times when our lives held no premium. We were having dinner one day at a place where two men had just been murdered. This frightened our soldiers to such an extent that we had to dismiss them and finish the trip without any natural protection. We passed places where thriving cities had been, but the Communists had burned them to the ground with many lives being lost. A number of days we were warned not to travel as the road was infested with robbers, but we traveled every day, except one, and then it was the rain that stopped us.

One morning, as we left a city, there was a mountain in front with alternate roads around it. We took the left-hand one while a large Chinese merchant caravan just behind us took the right.

At eleven a.m. they were attacked and robbed of their goods. What led us to take the left hand? We believe it was God. Another time, we passed a spot where the Chinese said the Reds had killed twenty-five men, and we were traveling in their direction. The Lord protected us, for we did not see any trace of them.

A very high mountain was to be scaled one day. We started early to ascend its heights. In about two hours the chief horseman came rushing back to us, pale and nervous. "Pastors, this mountain is full of brigands. Hasten the mules, and stay close together." As we were nearing the summit, Mr. Carter and I dismounted to drink from a spring, and walked on, chatting together. We turned a sharp curve around a huge boulder and there we saw three filthy, ragged men, with cruel scowling faces, sitting polishing their long shining rifles. "Brother Carter, the robbers!" "No doubt," he whispered. Without uttering a word the three men joined our caravan, walking behind us. The Chinese horsemen, who usually joke all the time, were silent and pale as death. We walked five minutes, ten minutes, fifteen, with those guns just behind us. One of the men finally spoke, "We want money." Our interpreter gave him what he asked for, then he put his hands to his mouth and screamed. The whole mountain resounded with his voice. On the next ridge came an answer, then these men walked away. As we rode forward, a sincere prayer was sent Heavenward, and we never met any more of these men. Hallelujah, for the Lord God Omnipotent reigneth! Who were the men you ask? We do not know, but this we do know, God brought us back in safety from a desperate, ungoverned, bandit-ridden land, in peace.

Chapter 8

SHANGHAI TO TIENTSIN
BY AIRPLANE

*T*HREE MONTHS to the day after sailing from Hong Kong we steamed back into the beautiful harbor, again viewing Victoria Peak, the green Gibraltar of British domain. Friends met us at the dock, happy over our safe return from war-torn Yunnan. The following day we had boarded a train for Canton, the true metropolis of China and her most characteristic Chinese city.

Canton boasts of a recorded history of 4,000 years, also of being the first Chinese city to make a treaty for foreign trade, and strange as it might seem, about 85% of all the Chinese outside China are of Cantonese descent. They seem the most intelligent, the most industrious, of the world travelers.

We had only had a few hours in the great city of Canton, then boarded a ferry and crossed the Chukiang River to make connection with a train for Fatshan.

A sight that no traveler ever forgets is Canton

Harbor. One third of the enormous population of Canton are born, reared and die on a sampan or junk. As you pass them with their week's washing hanging on a pole, children diving in the river for a bath, it gives you another view of China's life. Other spectacular sights were the large river boats, painted in bright colors, with a large eye painted on the prow to help see the way. As the vessels carry freight and passengers up country, through bandit and pirate-infested parts, machine guns can be seen in predominant places.

In the evening we arrived in Fatshan and enjoyed walking down the main business section, seeing the stores all decorated with Chinese hieroglyphics, the family having their evening meal in the doorway. The family cat is chained to a post mewing for a morsel to eat. No dogs are chained in China, they are scavengers of the gutter.

For one week we ministered in a beautiful brick church built under the direction of Miss Ledbetter, one of our pioneer missionaries. Great crowds thronged the auditorium. A revival spirit was present. Chinese Christians received the Holy Spirit, many sick in body received wonderful healing. There were staunch decisions for Christ each day. We rejoiced to see the number of young men taking a stand for Christ, as anti-foreign and communistic feelings are growing with a noticeable rapidity in the schools.

Leaving Fatshan, we journeyed back to Canton and from thence to Hong Kong again. While waiting a few days for a passage north, we had some very large and spiritual meetings in Kowloon once more. On September 25th we boarded a boat, and waving farewell to a host of friends, we steamed north to Shanghai. Three days later we entered the muddy Whampoo River and soon anchored off the jetty. After the interrogation of the custom officials, we found it was to late to catch our train for Tientsin. This was the last train to catch to make connections for our announced meetings. Mr. Carter said that we must not disappoint the people. Therefore we enquired about the plane service and found one scheduled to fly north the following morning. We purchased our tickets to go on it.

In our night's stay in Shanghai, the missionaries and other foreigners gathered in the guest home and we enjoyed a refreshing service together. We were privileged to meet some of the far interior missionaries from Kansu Province.

The following morning the Chinese steward opened the cabin door of the airplane, called for the passengers, showed us our seat and strapped us in. With a roar, the plane taxied clumsily down the runway; the aviator tested the engines; the monster motors gave a terrified growl and we were off.

92

As we had sent a telegram from Shanghai announcing our arrival, the missionaries met us at the airport. The following day meetings began in a hall seating about 400 people. As different kinds of advertisements were distributed concerning the meetings, the first afternoon's meeting was well attended by natives and foreigners. A great spirit of prayer and expectation prevailed among the people. One of the first things I noticed was the exceptional Chinese choir leader, in charge of the singing. He seemed to move the emotions of the people with the greatest ease. Normally, the Chinese sing our foreign tunes very poorly, but he led them with correctness and a real inspiration.

We decided that the supreme difficulty in speaking to the Chinese was getting their attention and then keeping it. Right at a tense moment of a call to the unconverted, or in the middle of what should be an interesting story, you will see one get up and leave, and a dozen follow. The Chinese women are especially talkative and restless. We resorted to different tactics to hold their attention. At times we rang the little desk bell, or pounded the pulpit furiously, clapped our hands together or spoke in an unusual tone of voice. Of course it would sound very strange to our congregations in the homelands, but seemed to be just the thing to do in China. I am sure the Lord answered prayer and rewarded the faithful labors of missionaries in this time of soul-reaping we had in Tientsin. There were from five to twenty-five people who came to receive Christ each invitation given. Mr. Baltau, the Pastor, said there were 105 who definitely decided for Christ in our one week's visit.

Many of the Chinese launched out deeper into spiritual life. Many who had been seeking the baptism of the Holy Spirit found their Pentecost. Missionaries told us that a few years ago this would have been impossible as people told terrible tales about missionaries, even going so far as to say that they were Government spies or witches. When they ventured out in the street the people mocked and called them foreign devils. Chinese who decided for Christ underwent terrible persecution from relatives and friends. Now it makes our hearts to rejoice to see doctors, lawyers, newspaper reporters, business men, students and housewives kneeling before the true God, confessing a life of sorrow and sin, then accepting peace for this life and a home eternal for the future. The first night of this campaign we received a letter from a Chinese man who wanted to know how many creations there were, why did God permit man to fall in Eden and many other questions, concluding his letter by signing himself "a one-fourth Christian." We did not answer the letter, but prayed. A few nights later I was asked to pray for a man who could speak English. It was the man who had written the letter. How changed he was. With tears of repentance he asked God's forgiveness. He promised to live right, if God would only break the awful opium habit that was binding him. Each night after this he attended the meetings and testified to a change in soul and body. Praise God.

We were asked to give one service over the local radio station. Mr. Carter gave the message which was interpreted into Chinese. The Sunday before our departure on Monday, a number of converts desired Christian baptism, so the pastor conducted an impressive baptismal service with each candidate promising the Lord to walk in newness of life.

In meeting the Chinese of different sections of China, it is of interest to note that they all have the same custom in their introductory remarks. He first bows, takes a personal card from his purse, and presenting it asks, "What is your name?" You answer, then ask, "And yours?" "How old are you?" he continues. You tell him, and ask him the same question. Next he asks you, "How many sons do you have?" "What! No wife and no boys, what a pity!" etc., etc.

While in Tientsin, we witnessed our first elaborate Chinese funeral service. It reminded one more of a coronation than a funeral. After a few days' feasting and ritual by the Buddhist priests, the procession came slowly out of the house with about thirty men carrying the casket, which had a beautiful decorated house built over it. En route to the burial ground the band, consisting of about ten instruments, went in advance. Four or five priests, dressed in flowing robes, followed these. Then came the chief mourner who would be the oldest man left in the home. He walks in the procession, being held up by two friends, screaming and crying. This is rigid Chinese etiquette as the chief mourner must show great sorrow. The casket followed this, then a number of funeral buggies or rickshaws came last. Everyone in the procession had on decorated uniforms for such an occasion.

Another interesting thing we noticed in Tientsin was the host of professional girl beggars, usually from eight to ten years old. They ran with all their might by the side of our moving rickshaw, jabbering, "Money, please, money." If you did not give them any they followed you for a while screaming at you.

Leaving Tientsin, we took a train for Kalgan, on the Mongolian border. En route we stopped a few hours at the Great Wall of China. This was one of the Old World wonders. A million men are supposed to have died in its construction. It is really a net-work of walls that wind about the mountains from Shangai Kwan to Tibet like a serpent. Watch towers are constructed about a hundred yards apart. It is said that word could come from Tibet to Peiping within a day. The wall which was built over 200 years before Christ is in remarkable preservation. Many wars between the Chinese and Tartars were fought on it.

Upon arriving in Kalgan, we found a very windy city with a frequency of dust storms which burned the face and chafed the lips. It is surrounded by ghastly naked mountains, with an open pass leading into the Gobi desert. This being the chief outlet from Mongolia to China, there were many Mongols roaming about. They were as strange looking a people as the hill tribes of Burma, with their large boots, decorative clothing and dirty skins.

We were happy to see a goodly number of missionaries present, some from the interior of Mongolia to participate in the ten days' special meetings to be conducted in Mr. Beruldsen's mission. Our hearts were made to rejoice and we felt repaid for our journey in a filthy train when Christ's Ambassadors spoke of their appreciation for our coming. Some stated they did not know how they could stand the spiritual darkness any longer without some special aid from God. The friends from Mongolia said they had not seen a white face for ten months, before coming to the capital, and they felt a great need of fellowship and inspiration. God bless those Light Bearers in dark inland Asia we pray!

It was at Kalgan that we had our first adventure on the back of a large dromedary. Camel trains are a common scene through this section.

We visited a mosque and saw the people prostrating to their deities, but were not allowed into the inner temple, because we did not care to remove our shoes. There was a Confucius temple on a hillside just outside the city which we visited. It was very old and renowned for its architectural beauty. After climbing the steep ascent, we saw fierce gods standing with swords drawn, with a serpent in hand, and a number of dragon heads protruding from the body ready to devour all who disobeyed his word or did not offer incense to appease his wrath. Nowhere could we find a god named the God of *Love* to comfort and bless the people.

While in Kalgan we began each day with a homey fireside Bible study. In the afternoon was a general meeting for the Chinese Christians, concluding the day with an evangelistic meeting. We were asked to speak in the different missions of the city, which we enjoyed doing. Kalgan seemed a difficult city to labor in; the powers of darkness were ever fighting to hold their victims. We were very grateful for those who received the Holy Ghost, one being the adopted daughter of one of the missionaries now being trained in a local Bible School. Among those who accepted Christ were two women school teachers who seemed to receive a real bright experience. We were especially glad as the Chinese women are very difficult to reach.

Another interesting decision was a man who had been released from prison that day and now desired to be set free spiritually. He prayed that God might break the opium habit and cleanse his heart. He could be seen in the congregation each night after this with a radiant smile of satisfaction. A young man from the Methodist Bible school came over one afternoon to be prayed for. A disease of the bone had attacked him and settled in his hip. He used a crutch besides someone assisting him to walk. We prayed for him and he walked a few steps saying the pain was gone. God really did a wonderful and complete work, for that night he testified of walking without crutch or assistance. He asked for prayer that he might receive the Holy Spirit. The next day he left for Mongolia to tell those people of that dark land what the Christ, Son of the Omnipotent God, can do.

As neither Mr. Carter nor I had any national bias, but love the children of the Kingdom of all nations, we next visited four Scandinavian missions between Kalgan and Peiping. The Scandinavians have proved themselves to be excellent missionaries. Their great vision and sincere hearts reap a wonderful harvest for the Master. While with them we were privileged to speak in a

Chinese college for young men, and about sixteen of the young men came to our next mission meeting and accepted Christ as their Savior.

Chapter 9

THE IMPERIAL CITY

PEIPING, the great Imperial City of North China, is known as one of the most attractive and interesting cities on the globe. Here you walk into a medieval world, and can go adventuring with Marco Polo. You are permitted to walk reverently through the ancient temples and palaces and feel their atmosphere of mystery. Peiping is unlike the treaty ports such as Shanghai with its imposing water-front and massive modern buildings, and far from being like poor backward Yunnan. One finds here the ancient Oriental life, with all its weird fascinations in its natural setting. It makes an Occidental gasp with wonder to look at the exquisite design with its flaming colors of red, green and gold on the architecture.

This historic city has been a center of political struggle for about 4,500 years, and oftentimes the capital of China. Its name suffered a change about as often as the dynasties, being recently changed from Peking to Peiping.

In the beautiful public library we saw the largest

book in the world. It was originally taken from the Emperor's palace in Jehul. It has 36,300 manuscript volumes which were copied by hand, bound in silk and are preserved in 6,000 camphor cases.

When riding through the Legations one day we saw the British Embassy, the oldest in Peiping. As we went into the drive a white wall could be seen with bullet holes torn in it. Large block letters were written across it, "Lest we forget." During The Boxer uprising of 1900, the Dowager Queen sought to kill all the foreigners in her realm. A few missionaries took refuge behind this wall. The Boxers were tearing it down with gun-fire when British troops came to the rescue. A few years later the Chinese suggested it be taken down, in order to forget the terrible tragedy, but the British Ambassador repainted the wall, then wrote those words on it, to remind them how terrible was war.

One morning a friend took us out to see the Altar and Temple of Heaven. Here the Emperor came to pay his yearly obeisance to Heaven, the only superior he acknowledged. In approaching the temple we drove down an avenue flanked with cedars nearly 1,000 years old. The altar is priceless, being made of pure white marble. Around the edge are great furnaces where animals were offered as a sacrifice during worship. The temple stands on a white marble foundation reached by four flights of steps. There are no images in this temple; it is all mystic worship.

We visited the Forbidden City of Peiping. This is one mile square and is surrounded by high walls with turrets at the corners. Walking through the great gates, we noticed about three thick walls before any of the main palaces were seen. The guide showed us the superb palaces with their gracefully carved roofs covered with burnished yellow tiles. We saw the nine dragon wall made of porcelain, the artificial rock gardens, the ivory tableaux on the wall studded with jewels, the longest painted picture in the world, being ten miles long, and the Queen's mirror some sixteen feet high.

The meetings in Peiping were divided between three groups of missions. The first services were with some American missionaries. God blessed in an encouraging way. The afternoon services were splendid with nearly a full hall of Chinese Christians and missionaries. Many spoke of the blessing they received from these meetings. In the evening, special effort was put forth to touch the hearts of the unconverted. There were some who took a stand for Christ and came forward for prayer at each call. The next services were for some British missionaries conducted in a large rented picture palace which was packed out. Some were baptized with the Holy Spirit and others saved in these times of refreshing. Our last meetings were with the Swedish friends. It is quite different in China to what it is in the homeland. Sinners do not cross the city to find the Gospel Hall. We go to their neighborhood and seek to get them interested.

A woman came one night to the front weeping. She said, "I am a Christian, but my physician says he cannot heal me, and now I must die." We told her Christ would heal her. The ailment was a spinal trouble. We prayed and the pain left the woman, and the next night her face was bright and smiling as she told the missionary that she was completely healed and that she had not had a pain that day. Praise Jesus.

Our hearts were made to rejoice at the reception the people gave God in Peiping and other cities, as it is apparent that permanent trouble is brewing in the East. Many of the far inland missionaries of the north have had to evacuate their mission stations, many suffering hardships getting to the coast, such as floating on a goat skin raft for a few weeks. The Communists have taken their province and are murdering and stealing as they like, the missionaries being a prized prey in their path of destruction.

As we pulled out of Tientsin for Manchuria on the Japanese express train, a great feeling of completeness in seeing Asia's Middle Kingdom was ours.

We had sat on the back of a mule on a lonely Yunnan mountain slope and gazed over into tropical Burma. From Chu Tien we had looked with interest toward the wild desolate country of Tibet. On the powerful little mountain train we have ridden through the towering hilltops that divide China from French Indo-China. By boat, train, and airplane we travelled the coast length of China. Standing on the great wall of China, we were privileged to look right into the dark, mystical land of Mongolia, beholding the very places where battles raged between the primitive Mongols and the crafty Chinese 500 years before the herald angels announced the glad tidings of Emmanuel.

Chapter 9

THE LAND OF RISING TROUBLE

JAPAN is one of the nerve centers of the modern world, and probably one of the most watched countries of today. Statesmen keep an ever watchful eye on her as she intriguingly plays her role in the world's great political drama. Many are having qualms of terror as she daringly claims to be mistress of sea and land at such a startling rapidity. Manufacturers lose sleep watching her because she fills the world's markets with all kinds of merchandise at ridiculously low prices. Hundreds of occidental owned factories in China, Manchuria, and in the homelands are being unmercifully pushed to the rocks by her.

Pleasure seekers look admiringly toward Japan because it is one of the most famous playgrounds of the world. Its scenery is hardly surpassed, and it is with pride and efficiency that Japan caters to tourists from all over the world. Christianity, too, with a wistful eye looks to see signs of a spiritual revival along with the national revival. Without a doubt, Japan has been in the midst of a mighty national awakening for nearly two-thirds of a century.

As a matter of personal opinion, after visiting her largest cities and also small towns, I concluded that the Western World had given Japan a wonderful modern civilization and had brought her from oblivion into the limelight, but we have miserably failed in giving her Christianity. I should think Japan with all her enlightenment and progress is one of the most difficult fields for successful missionary activity.

A major reason is that Christendom offered her a social gospel in the beginning. They built hospitals, orphanages, and colleges, but left Christ in the background, and there He still stays! Social welfare and Christian education are gracious fruits of Christianity, but when Christ the Savior is presented first, in His rightful place, these graces follow in indigenous channels which are their correct and most appreciated spheres. Another great reason would be the strict nationalistic training of the Japanese from their babyhood, to worship the Emperor first, above all.

One of our missionary friends said that he had a young Japanese man converted in his meetings. As he was intelligent and seemed very interested in soul-winning, he started training him to be an evangelist. One day this English missionary and his Japanese evangelist were talking about the death of King George V. The Japanese said, "But you know your King was only a man." "Yes," replied the missionary, "rulers are fallible and mortal just as we are." "No, no," quickly responded the Japanese, "our Emperor is a god." The missionary said, "Why, you know your Emperor is no more a god than our King." "Yes," shouted the Japanese, "He is a god; we worship him." The missionary tried in vain to reason with him. He said, "Brother, Jesus is the only God we are allowed to worship. He is the true and Living God." The evangelist said, "Well, I will not preach in your church any more." So he gave up his position as an evangelist to worship the Mikado.

In our visit to Japan we began meetings in Tokyo and worked south. Our first meetings were in the Takingogawa Church and Bible School. The Principal dismissed the regular classes of the school and brought the students together to hear Mr. Carter's lectures. The Japanese students seemed to greatly enjoy the daily visit to the fountain of Spiritual Gifts, as Brother Carter also enjoyed leading them there. The evening services were mostly made up of missionaries and Japanese Christians who were hungry for the Word. There were not very many unconverted people attending the meetings, but most of those who did were convicted of their sins and accepted Christ. Adding to the joy of these meetings, there were those who sought for a deeper spiritual life, and found it in the Holy Spirit.

Mr. Carter and I thought the Japanese mannerisms quite interesting. No street shoes are to be worn in the house or church; at the door you are asked kindly to remove them. The porch or vestibule of the church looked like a second hand shoe shop. Even in places like barber shops your shoes have to be taken off and a pair of soft slippers are supplied you while you get a haircut or shave.

A kind friend duly informed us that before beginning a discourse we should bow to the congregation and then at the end bow again, and the audience returns the courtesy. When we first arrived in Japan and saw the formal introductions it was very amusing. Two people meet, stand facing each other, then start bowing low and looking into the face of the other and greeting them. They bow from three to seven or eight times. To see some thirty or forty couples going up and down as a train arrives or leaves a station is a sight for a westerner. In meeting we were told to make just one polite bow to the men or women, and to refrain from shaking hands. It all seemed very strange and sometimes we unthinkingly put out our hand instead of bowing.

When we arrived in Tokyo our hostess asked me if I would care for a bath. The maid prepared one. I was given the needed directions not to bath in the large wooden barrel, but in the small wooden basin, then get in the barrel and soak for some twenty or thirty minutes. I was enjoying the new style bath. After some ten minutes my body began to tingle, then the water began to steam. What was it all about? In a few minutes I was nearly burning up. Jumping out of the tub, I found a furnace underneath. Slowly I was being boiled alive! After this, I saw to it that the hidden stoves were not burning.

We were told that the reason you did not bathe in the large barrel was that all the family used the same water. While visiting an orphanage home near Kobe, I took my bath on Christmas Eve in the same water that twenty-four others had just finished with.

From Tokyo, we went to Tachikawa, a suburban city. The missionary here was engaged in children's educational work and also had a Gospel Hall. On both nights of our visit, sinners accepted Christ, and the Christians testified to blessings. From here we visited Yabo for one night. The hall was packed. The missionary stated that divine healing had caused the growth of this work. One woman had been healed of a stroke; an elderly man had been healed of rheumatism. It all happened through the Christians praying for one another. The lady missionary also pointed out a woman who was found trying to commit suicide in a cemetery when a Christian found her and told her about God's love for sinners. She accepted Christ and now is one of the strongest members in the church.

Our next meetings were in Sugamo Church. The Japanese pastor seemed very enthusiastic about our coming to this chapel, and later stated that he had received a new and larger vision of the spiritual needs of Japan. Our last meetings in this section were in Yokohama with Mr. N. Barth of the U.S.A. There were a number who confessed their lost condition, which is very hard for an oriental person to do.

Itinerating in Japan is not primitive in the least. Courtesy, service, comfort, all are given with a charm that is peculiar to themselves. The passing scenery was wonderful. One might see a beautiful orchard of ripe luscious citrus fruit with the famous Mount Fuji, Japan's sacred snow-capped mountain, holding its head high above the floating clouds as a background. Or you may see a farmer in his field plowing with an ox and one-handled wooden plow, while speeding past him will be the latest model motor-car.

The most obnoxious cruelty to the women of the Orient is found in Japan's "licensed quarters." It is a governmental system licensing prostitutes, and they live in colonies about the city. In most cases the owner of a licensed house will tour the poor farmers' and peasants' homes and make bids for their daughters. These simple country folk sell their beautiful virtuous girls into these veritable hells for a small sum of money. Sometimes a daughter is sold in order to help educate a son. Taken from their simple rural life, the slave master takes them to his brothel and a life of sin, misery, disease and death follows. Many of these girls commit suicide each year, as life is unbearable for them.

The geisha girl is marked. She cannot dress as an ordinary person, but must fix her hair in a certain fashion. Their ornaments and make-up are different from every other woman. We have seen them come in and sit down on a streetcar and a respectable citizen will move away at once, as it is a disgrace to associate with them. What many a heartache they must suffer.

From Central Japan, we came south to Hamamatsu, the musical city. Here most of the musical intruments of Japan are manufactured. We visited one of the largest factories and saw them turning out pianos for the American market. The guide who was showing us through demonstrated his newest invention, an organ without pipes, and he told us where he received the idea. In a large Catholic cathedral in Tokyo a new organ arrived from Italy. It was a new type. Our guide said he played an organ well, so he went up and begged permission to play it and to hear how it sounded. He told us that while playing it he looked inside at the works, came back to his factory, drew the blueprint, and now Japan can sell them to Italy cheaper than she can produce them. This reveals how Japan imitates the world. Speaking of business tactics, some very comical things can be seen in Japan. A tailor shop, seeking Christians and missionaries to trade there, put up a sign which read, "Buy your pants here, they warm your legs like the love of God."

In Mamamatsu the missionary, Miss A. Juergensen, and a native evangelist had the meetings well announced, and we were pleased to see the mission hall nearly full each night. The missionary reported twelve decisions for Christ. Our next stop was at the fast-growing seaport city of Nagoya. While here, it snowed and turned bitterly cold. We preached twice in this place. Then from here we took the train down to the old, weird and fascinating city of Kyoto. For a thousand years it was the capital of Japan. It is famous for its magnificent palaces and temples.

We were delighted to minister here to an indigenous church. It was in a healthy condition and about as strong in attendance as any we visited in Japan. The first night Mr. Ogawa, the teacher, with another teacher from a self-supporting church in Osaka, desired Brother Carter to ordain them officially as pastors. They had served in the ministry for some years. The ordination service was very precious; the young men received helpful instructions as to their duty to the Church and toward Christ. It was very encouraging to see the Japanese Christians come through rain and snow to attend the services, especially as they have no stoves in their churches. A porcelain firepot or two in the aisle, which only warms the fingers of those sitting nearest, is all the fire the Japanese use. When we heard them pray and saw their faces beam with the gospel light, it assured us that they really knew Jesus Christ. We were also invited to the fellowship house in Kyoto for a foreign service with some Japanese students. We realized most of them came to hear English spoken, but we pray that God pricked their hearts with His divine truth, and that eternal results will follow that service.

Osaka, Japan's greatest industrial city, was our next scene of revival effort. Miss Oki, who is the daughter of an ex-mayor of Osaka, is the founder of the church we ministered in. When she accepted Jesus Christ as her Savior, her parents disinherited her and she was obliged to leave home, but thanks be to God, our Heavenly Father took her in and gave her a prosperous church to pastor.

Miss Oki prepared the famous Sukiyaki feast for us one evening. As the Japanese do not have chairs in their homes or churches, we sat on the straw mat floor around a table some eight inches high. The various kinds of food were brought in, all on one plate. A little portable gas stove was placed on the table and the maid began cooking our food before our eyes. When you saw a piece of meat or some vegetable that looked tasty, you put your chopsticks into the pan and took it out. If it was too hot, a raw egg in a saucer was at our side in which we dipped it to cool it. We enjoyed the feast each meeting, God blessing our united efforts in a definite way.

During the New Year holidays, we were at Ikoma in a large convention. Koreans, Japanese and a number of missionaries were present. Three great meetings each day were held.

Our concluding meetings in Japan were in the city of Kobe and vicinity. The Door of Hope Mission, whose activities many have read about for the last twenty years, was the scene of special meetings. Many fallen girls have been rescued through the influence of this mission, and given a new start in life. On our last Sunday, the Union Church of Kobe for foreigners invited Mr. Carter to be the speaker. It really seemed strange, but delightful, to be in a large western designed church and to hear English hymns and prayers. The change almost seemed as if we had been transplanted to our homeland for a brief space of time.

Like a fantastic dream of the night, our labors in Japan hastened to a close. After eight weeks and two days in this wonderful little island empire of the East, we were standing on the railway platform with a group of Christian friends. After wishing them the greatest of success in this land of spiritual darkness, we boarded the Shimonoseki express for Korea. One farewell wave and we were out of their sight. In the afternoon we were riding alongside the Inland Sea which prominent writers describe as one of the most glorious sights in the world. Its little green turfed islets and deep blue waters seem to transport one to a dreamland. So on we went towards Korea.

The roar of rushing wheels and the movements of the flying express train awakened me before time to arise next morning. I pulled the curtain to one side, and from the carriage window I received my first impression of the Land of the Morning Calm. It was a humorous sight that met my eyes and very different to any we had seen in other countries.

There were a number of men walking down the highway in the Oriental trot as it was a very cold morning. On the men's heads were the famous top-knot hats and ball of hair, that the Korean gentle-men of the last generation thought very stately. Their clothes were all white, and this being the winter season their baggy trousers were padded and tied around the ankles, somewhat like the Chinese. Their overcoat was a long white affair. It was rather strange to see the men and women dressed in white making their way over to the river to cut the next summer's supply of ice. While speaking of dress, we thought the little Korean girls dressed most attractively, especially on festive occasions. They wore dazzling colors, jackets of bright red, skirts of bright green and sometimes their dress sleeves would look like a rainbow with all colors in them.

On down through Korea we traveled, until late in the afternoon we arrived at the capital city of Seoul. Two of Mr. Carter's former Bible school students from England are doing missionary work here. They met us at the station with a number of local Christians. As in Japan, bowing is the formal greeting. When we arrived at the house where we were to stay, again we were asked to kindly remove our shoes. It is a great offence in the eyes of the Koreans to wear dirty shoes in a clean house.

On the first evening of our arrival we attended a service. When we came to the door of the church and opened it, we were startled, for all the people were sitting on the floor with little straw mats under them. We entered, followed the usual custom, pulled off our shoes and exchanged a few courtesies. We were pleased to see they had a chair for each of us, as it would have been very difficult to sit on our feet for an hour or more. We soon saw that the people had a living experience of true Christianity. On the next day, being Sunday, three

117

meetings were held. It was a great pleasure to speak to the Koreans as they sat still and listened attentively. After the evening meeting, nine decided for Christ. One night in a meeting I said, "Now I will tell you a story," and my Korean interpreter said, "Now I will tell you a *lie.*" A missionary very kindly helped us through the situation.

A man who had not walked outside his yard for four years was brought to a meeting and prayed for. God healed him, and the next day he walked down to the station to see us off. His wife received the Holy Spirit in the same meeting, so they now rejoice together in the blessings of God. Another man, who had been mentally deranged for the last two years and had lost his position, after being prayed with, his mental balance was perfectly restored and his former employer placed him in his old position. There were other healings of different kinds that strengthened the faith of the saints and made sinners to see the power of Jehovah.

Our visit seemed all too brief to these people. A number came down to the station to see us off to Manchuria, and sang and prayed in the old-fashioned way, as the train pulled out.

Chapter 11

MANCHUKUO

IT was midnight and we were sleeping soundly as the express train just crossed the Korea-Manchuria border and the Japanese officials awakened us for immigration procedure. Soon it was all finished, we passed the border city of Antung, and then went flying on into the night. In the late afternoon of the same day we arrived in Port Arthur, Kwantung, the territory Japan received as a war indemnity from defeated Russia. Now we were in Japan's puppet State to conduct meetings. Manchukuo is a very large territory, north of China, south of Siberia, with Korea on the east side and Mongolia on the west. Her five provinces contain an area larger than France, Germany, Switzerland and Austria combined.

We had arrived in Port Arthur on the Chinese New Year (Lunar Calendar). Again we were to minister to the Chinese people (the natives of Manchuria are Chinese) and at the greatest festive time of their year. Today was *everybody's* birthday. In China births are not recorded in July, September, etc., but years are added on the first day of the year. The Chinese have a very strange custom, the day a baby is born it is one year old. If they are born on the 31st day of December, the next day, on January 1st, they are not only two days old, but also two years old! At this season the Chinese are turned to reveling for the next fifteen or sixteen days. There is to be no work or worry to hinder their jubilee feasting and worshiping holiday. All the Chinese who can possibly afford one get a new outfit. It is customary to pay up all outstanding debts and to give gifts to friends. The ladies set a feast before the men that will not be seen again until next New Year's day. At this season they tear down all their paper gods and place up new ones. The god of the kitchen gets a small piece of paper pasted over his mouth before he is torn down, so that he will not be able to tell any bad tales about what he has seen or heard during this brief ministry of one year. Thousands of little home and roadside shrines are decorated with bright red paper with large black hieroglyphics on them. As you pass along the road you can see the incense sticks burning and little piles of grain or dishes of food being offered up to the gods. The Chinese are very anxious to start the New Year with favor from their gods.

We saw and visited hundreds of shrines, temples, and lamaseries while in the Orient. It was heartrending to see the poor deceived people sincerely praying to gods of mud, wood and stone. In the temple of 500 disciples of Buddha in Yunnan province, we saw the great gold-covered Buddha surrounded by 500 idols, which were grotesque, devilish and absurd. One god held the sun in his hand, another gave baby boys to mothers, another ruled hell, and so on. Nowhere could a God of love and compassion be found.

Yet thanks be to God, all the Chinese are not taken up with the heathen festival, nor with the worshiping of idols.

On New Year's night we had a nice audience, and when the plea for the unconverted was given, about twenty knelt to begin the New Year with Jesus as their Savior.

Our five days visit in Port Arthur were days of divine visitation. We were delighted to see the marked success of the lady missionaries laboring here. The station had been opened only about two years, and they now have a beautiful nucleus of believers.

From Port Arthur, we journeyed north to Mukden, one of the greatest cities in Manchuria for industry and commercial life. Our meetings had been very uncertain here owing to the Japanese purge. Many local Christians had been imprisoned as anti-Japanese instigators. This made people afraid to go to church. We were welcomed to

Mukden by a group of friendly missionaries and an enthusiastic group of Christians. The beautiful new stucco tabernacle, seating over 250 people, was full for the opening service. A delightful spiritual move was felt from the beginning; the first service ended with a few new faces at the front seeking God. A special healing service was announced for the second day, and a great number came forward to be healed of all kinds of ailments and troubles. The poor Chinese can have the most terrible dirty diseases, but God was present with mercy and power.

A number testified to a definite touch from God. One woman came up limping on her crutch, one leg badly deformed. After being prayed for she jumped up and left her crutch, walked about the church and then to her home praising God for His power to heal. The missionary in charge, Brother Kvamme, had been ill previous to our coming and had to live on a special diet. During the first service, while interpreting for Brother Carter, he received a great blessing and all his pains vanished. From this time he ate anything he desired and suffered no more pains.

Each meeting in Mukden was a scene of revival and blessing, but when one asked for the unconverted to come forward we found the Christians came as well. Along the altar many times could be seen little pools of tears, which the missionary stated was a rare thing among the Chinese, and showed a truly broken spirit.

The day before we left Mukden an unconverted man who lived near the church died. The family sent for the musicians, who sat in the gateway playing weird unearthly music on a Chinese instrument, while another sang. In the afternoon there appeared a great paper horse of diverse colors and a paper cart. This was in order that the man's spirit would not have to walk on his journey through the spiritual world. That night we looked in at the front door. They had candles lit on a table, with a number of different kinds of food before them. At one end of the coffin were five or six dishes of food for the dead, which the priests ate themselves while talking all the time to the dead man. Our hearts cried unto God, "Oh Lord, how long before these benighted souls shall see Your light and truth and accept it?"

From Mukden we went north again to Harbin, the great cosmopolitan city of Manchuria, in which we found Russians, Germans, Polish, Japanese and Chinese, besides about 250 English-speaking people. It was bitter cold; the river was frozen to a depth that large trucks were able to pass over on the ice. Another glimpse of Chinese wretchedness was seen on arrival here. People were lying along the street dead, frozen to death. The beggars had stolen their clothes while another had kicked them to one side to let the traffic pass. We asked why they were not taken up, and were told, "Oh, next spring they will be put on carts and taken outside the city and burned." Beggar women, sometimes with a child in their arms, could be seen on the streets two-thirds naked, shaking with cold and dying with hunger, screaming to the passers-by for a few pennies with which to buy opium.

We were told in Mukden that our last place to visit in Manchuria would be the cream of the itinerary. To our joy we did find a lovable and receptive group of Chinese who seemed to have a real hunger for spiritual things. Most of the Christians being business people and having a fair education, they could understand biblical truths without difficulty. The meetings had a delightful freedom in them, some receiving the Holy Spirit and others salvation. While in Harbin we were invited to minister at the Russian Eastern European Mission Station. The fellowship was very precious in the three meetings. Most of the people were emigrants, who had been banished from home by the Bolshevik reign in Russia. To look at them made one feel sad; they had such expressions of grief and hardness of countenance that results from much trouble and privation. When preaching to them, however, we found tender hearts. About ten decided for Christ with tears of repentance during our stay.

This ended our visit to the Orient. The moving millions of Chinese we should see no more on this visit. Thus we left the people where dessert comes first at the meal, where the masculine dress is of silk and women wear trousers, where a man shakes his own hand in introduction and his surname comes first. Yes, a land of many interesting diverse customs to ours, but with it all they found a close place in our hearts and prayers. God bless China and all the Orient!

Chapter 12

THROUGH SIBERIA AND RUSSIA

IT was in the Russian Consulate at Harbin, Manchuria, that Mr. Carter and I were seeking a transit visa or permit to cross Siberia and Russia to Poland. Our passports were ready to be endorsed when the consul did not quite understand the word "minister." He said, "Are you missionaries or the like?" "Yes, we are engaged in missionary work." "Well, we will have to wire to Moscow to get special permission for you to pass through the Soviet Union. The telegram will take two or three weeks to receive a reply and cost you $18." "Do you mean," we asked, "that because we are ministers of the gospel we cannot travel as ordinary tourists?" "Yes, you will have to get a special permit from Moscow; it is nothing personally that you have done, it is only you are preachers and this is our law!"

As much as twice a day for the next five days we were obliged to call in at the consulate for some particulars. The British consul and the American consul both called on the U.S.S.R. consulate to try and hasten things up as we had meetings booked on the Continent, but had no success. Eventually permission was received, but we had to postpone dates through the long delay.

We took a train from Harbin to Manchouli, the Siberian frontier station. En route I conversed with the chief steward of the dining car who was a Russian. He told me that the people were taught that there is no God right from babyhood. This had dealt a deadly blow to the morals of the younger generation. They fear no divine retribution upon them, no coming judgment day, therefore they live lives of debauchery and shame. They have eliminated all holy matrimonial ceremonies. If a man and a woman visit the recording office together and sign their names, they are considered man and wife. If they agree to part, one of them can appear and have it annulled and all is completed for a few cents.

I shall not soon forget the morning when I looked out of the compartment window of the train and had my first full view of Russo-Siberia. There was a large crimson flag hoisted above the station where we had stopped. I noticed three large glaring portraits hanging in predominant places on the station. They bore cruel expressions of ferocity and subtlety. The side ones were Marx and Lenin, and the one in the center Stalin. We saw these same portraits on many stations in Russia. Around the

127

little log station were a number of people poorly clad and with an expression of deep depression and privation written across their brows. Behind the station were a few log huts. We were now in the wilds of Siberia.

It might be of interest to know what we paid for food in Russia. A four-course dinner came to $5.00 (£1). A lemonade or cup of tea bought separately was 50 and 60 cents (2s. to 2s. 6d.).

We felt that we were being shadowed by a member or members of the O.G.P.U. which has been changed to N.K.V.D. of late years. We believe that we were possibly detained in Harbin so that a special detective could come and escort us across. This Russian secret police is said to be the largest and most dangerous in the world. The man you work with or a member of your own family might be a N.K.V.D. agent. If you spoke against Communism or Stalin you would die without even a trial to defend yourself. This devilish spy system has brought thousands of innocent people to face a firing squad or Siberian exile. There was a brutal looking figure who delighted in standing around our door, and he slept in the next compartment. He would strain his eyes to see what we were reading, or strain an ear to hear a word of conversation, but not one word of English could he understand or speak if we spoke to him. There was an English missionary lady about three or four coaches behind us, and we went back to talk with her a few times. As soon as we did a Russian appeared and stood in the doorway until we left. I am sure he could tell by our actions that his presence was not desired, yet he persisted in hearing all that we said.

We passed a crew of logmen working by the railway. As the train was going very slowly we could see them distinctly. Their faces showed strain and fatigue. They were poorly dressed in rough, ragged clothes. On one side stood a well-dressed soldier with his rifle, watching them work. Our train thermometer registered forty to fifty degrees below zero. Yes, no doubt it was a camp of exiles suffering the terrible hardships of a Siberian forester. It could easily have been a group of our own Christian brethren, exiled for Christ's sake. A friend of ours was crossing the U.S.S.R. when they stopped at a station alongside another freight train. The latter was going east into Siberia loaded with human cargo, herded like cattle. Someone in the train called to the station master that there was a dead woman among the exiles going to the concentration camp. They asked him to remove her. He replied, "I would not care a d__ if you were all dead," and the train pulled out with a dead woman in their carriage. A sample of Bolshevic love.

The lady missionary, traveling alone, was surprised to see a big Russian brute of a man put in her coupe to sleep. He came in late in the night. This so frightened the lady that she stood out in a cold corridor the rest of the night. Communism does not have any respect for women folk. Many times we thought how hard Communism was on the opposite sex, as about 90 per cent of the snow-diggers and railway yard workers were poorly clad, undernourished, haggard-looking women. We saw hundreds of little dugouts or caves in the snow with a log roof over them. This was home for the Siberian peasant.

We passed through great cities and open prairies, over high mountains and through deep valleys. Seven days after leaving Manchouli and traveling through a wilderness of snow and ice, Moscow, the Imperial City, loomed up before us. To the casual traveler she is only the Russian metropolis but Moscow to the Russian is the sacred city. It is the Mecca of Socialism, the Jerusalem of Communism. Russians save money a lifetime to pay homage here for a few days. In the pre-revolution days Moscow was known as a city of churches, there being 1,600 in her precincts. Today she is known as the capital of the godless.

As we had about five hours to wait here, we took a taxi in order to see a little of the city. We saw the large apartment houses for the Government employees. Each had a crimson flag hoisted over them. We came to the Soviet Square and Statue of Liberty where the great revolution of October, 1917, commenced. From here we drove into the famous Red Square. We could scarcely believe that we were standing in the square which for hundreds of years has been an execution ground. If these cobble stones could relate the history of Russia, their eloquence would be a hideous nightmare. During the 1917 revolution this square flowed with human blood. "The price of freedom," Lenin cynically said. To our right rose a grandstand of stone seats. In the center is a red granite mausoleum. This is the Bolshevic shrine, where hundreds and thousands come to pay homage to the person who "rid the earth of the Czars." Inside in a glass casket lies embalmed a man with small iron features. Since February 1, 1924, his earthly activity has ceased. Near to the place where Lenin lies cold, still and pale, he once lifted his right hand and told God Almighty he would "brain Him." We were shown the numerous muscums, including the anti-religious museum which was formerly a place of worship. Here the artists have depicted God as a fun-looking fool, smoking a pipe, sitting up on top of the people. Jesus Christ is shown as a hideous criminal holding a sword dripping with blood in one hand and some bloody human skulls in the other. This has been Russia's education for her children now for twenty years.

The Russian utopia is a failure, but there cometh One who shall reign as King of kings, in a reign of righteousness. Prosperity shall be universal. Peace shall cover the entire earth, and our prayers should be "Thy Kingdom come."

Chapter 13

ITINERATING IN POLAND

WHAT a relief! We were at last out of the land of spies and suspicion. Nine days after pulling out of Harbin, Manchuria, we crossed the Russo-Polish border into the land of the "Children of the Sun." At Stalpse, the Polish border town, we bade farewell to the trans-Siberian express and all of Red Russia. To our joy we were met here by Mrs. Bergholc, a former student of the Bible school at Louth, England, and she escorted us the rest of the journey to Lodz. In this ancient Polish city, with its buggy taxis, cobblestone streets, we were met and welcomed by Mr. Bergholc, who had been a student of Mr. Carter's Bible school in London. He had planned a great Bible conference during our visit to his assembly. Twenty-five visiting pastors were present. It was truly an inspiration to be in Christian meetings again and to enjoy the warm fellowship of our beloved Polish brethren.

Our meetings could not be advertised on billboards or newspapers as the government is antagonistic to special campaigns. Walking to church on our first Sunday morning, Brother Carter and I noticed many people dressed in their best clothes, going to places of worship. We inquired if the Lord's day was officially set apart by the government and were told that it was. No shops were allowed to be opened for business on Sundays. This was our first real Sunday since we had left Australia over a year ago. All the far eastern countries disregarded Sunday. The gods of the heathen do not give their worshippers one day out of the seven to rest.

There were three meetings a day in the church while we were in Lodz. Morning and afternoon were devoted to Bible teaching. During the evening meetings the people were often seen to be whispering to one another. Some did not understand Polish, and others not German, therefore a kind friend had to sit by the side of the unfortunate listeners and interpret the sermon for them. In spite of the obstacles put in the way of advertising the meetings, people came from far and near, and on Sunday night the auditorium was packed and some of the people had to go into an ante-room. There were those who took a firm stand for Christ and those who received a touch of the mighty quickening Spirit.

Poland is the home of a few million of Abraham's descendants. It was most interesting to see Jews do everything from sweeping the streets to owning the largest factories in the country. The Polish Jew does not become a member of the local society like the English or American Jew. He wears his long beard, his little Jewish black cap and quaint dress.

The final day in Lodz came all too soon. Our next meetings in Poland were far into the eastern section among the white Russians in the town of Wilno. We were given a hearty welcome by the brethren. The first evening we were asked to speak to the Jews in the Jewish mission of the R.E.E.M. The next day we were taken about the city to see a few places of interest. We walked up the Holy Street where every man has to remove his hat or pay a fine. We saw the noted Ostra Brama Cathedral which is built over the street. In the front, directly above the street, is the famous and magnificent painting of the Virgin Mary. Her apparel is sewn with threads of gold. Here the priest ministers at the altar while the people kneel in the street below. Heavy snow was on the ground, but this did not deter the people from worshipping before this picture. When one considers that the Roman Catholics compose 85 per cent to 87 per cent of the population of Poland, it gives cause to shout for joy to know that the R.E.E.M. has over twenty thousand converts who will not bow their knees to this idolatrous church.

The meetings in the local assembly at Wilno were full of blessing. The saints here liked very long services. After eight or ten hymns and a lengthy prayer three speakers usually ministered. At the close of the Sunday evening meeting twelve decisions were recorded for the Kingdom.

On March 17th we took the train for Olechnowicze. We arrived at the nearest station at five-thirty the following morning. Stanislav Niedzviecki, the senior missionary in this district, met us. He lived eight miles from the railway station, therefore we had to ride this distance in a Russian springless wagon. The road, if it could be called such, was terrible, and we only had a little straw beneath us for a cushion. As we drove along it seemed at times that the wagon would turn over when we hit the large holes. We noticed at all the crossroads en route large wooden crosses, on each of which was nailed a small metallic crucifix very weather-beaten. After two hours of terrific bumping, we reached the missionaries' home. It was on the Russian border, and his house stood about two hundred yards from the sentry post. In the evening we had an enjoyable meeting. The Russians sang their deep melancholy songs with an original rhythm.

In the afternoon of the following day we once more went by horse and wagon thirteen miles to Ludwiene. We arrived about five-thirty, and after a Russian supper we went to the little log church. It was packed with people, whose anxious faces showed their eagerness to hear the word. The leader said it had been four years since a visiting minister had last been with them. Here about twelve decided to become disciples of Christ, which made our hearts rejoice.

The next morning after having shared our bed, which was about eight inches too short, with a number of unwelcome bedmates, we had a Russian breakfast, which consisted of a boiled egg, black bread and tea. After the meal we had a meeting for the Christians and workers, some of whom had walked over twenty-one miles to get there. In fact we got out and walked the last two and half miles, with the result that when we arrived, tired and hungry, a two-room log cabin seemed to us like a palace, and the coarse Russian food a feast. The friends had prepared us a Russian bath, but when we looked into the barn and saw its dirty floor and hot stones on which they were to throw water to create a vapour bath, we decided it best not to have one.

In the evening the hall was packed to suffocation, with many standing. Some of the Christians had made themselves crude stringed instruments from which, however, emanated delightful music. After four or five speakers had given messages, a number of the unsaved gave themselves to Christ.

That night there were four of us men and one woman sleeping in the same room. There were only two rooms to the house. The family slept on the top of the large Russian stove which was made for the purpose.

Another wagon ride and then 170 miles by train brought us to Baranowicze. The missionary in charge of the assembly here met us, his face beaming with the anticipation of God's blessing during our stay. The hall was crowded at the morning and evening services. Brother Myshak had not received the baptism of the Holy Spirit, so Mr. Carter prayed with him and God gave the blessing of Pentecost.

Our next meetings were at Sielce. Here we found a building seating about two hundred and fifty people. Since the village had taken a holiday to see the foreigners, the hall was overcrowded at the first service. It was inspiring to look into the eager smiling faces. All the women wore plataks on their heads, a kind of kerchief made of bright colors that fairly gleamed in the sunlight. Some of the men wore crude handmade foot gear of strips of bark from the trees. But despite the poverty, God's presence was very real, and the hallelujahs which came spontaneously from these happy Christians, caused us to rejoice. In the evening service we had many hymns and four sermons, and some sinners came to Jesus.

Twenty miles again by wagon brought us to another village for more meetings. This place had never been visited before by a foreign preacher, consequently everyone got into the hall who possibly could, and about twenty-five made the decision to follow Christ. Then, on another sixteen miles toward a distant village. During the last five miles we encountered a snow storm with a strong east wind which turned the weather bitterly cold. Our fur coats were lifesavers in the open wagon on such occasions. Arriving at our destination, we found the usual crowds. The people were hungry for the Word of God. The building, with seating capacity of 200, had three hundred packed into it. At the close of the meeting about thirty Christians followed us to our lodgings desiring to be prayed for. After a few minutes rest and a glass of warm milk, we resumed our wagon journey. We arrived at a railway station just after daybreak tired and nearly frozen from an icy rain that had fallen during the night. Here we took the train for Krzemieniec, which we reached about midday. When we arrived, the kind hostess, realizing where we had been, asked that she be allowed to prepare us a hot bath, and wash our soiled clothes. When she saw our woollen underwear, she said, "Just what I expected, covered with nests of lice." Although we had not realized their presence, we were relieved to be clean again. The meetings here were blessed by God and a number were converted.

A motor-car ride of sixty-five miles, and then by train for a further nine miles, brought us to another church. When we arrived we found the building and ante-room packed with happy Christians singing the songs of Zion. The pastor said some of them had walked sixty-five miles to attend this Bible conference. It was marvelous how these people worshipped God in such freedom in the Spirit. Glory filled their souls, and the Holy Spirit descended and Pentecost was again repeated. When I asked where all the visiting people found lodgings, we were told by the pastor that about one hundred slept on the floor of the mission hall, with only a bit of straw under them. They had walked as far as sixty-five miles in snow, some of them wearing shoes made from strips of bark from willow trees, and stockings made of rags wrapped around their legs. As long as their souls caught a spark from off the heavenly altar they did not worry about cold weather, black bread or a bed.

We boarded a train for our last appointment in Poland. Arriving in Pelczanka, we had the pleasure of ministering to the German colonists here for two days. Our Polish ministry concluded in this town. We felt it had been the hardest and most tiring itinerary of the world tour, but it was also one of continued blessing. Over a hundred miles by springless wagon, sitting on a little bag of hay, food beyond digestion, or even lice is nothing when we can be a blessing to even one of God's children. At the large Warsaw central station we waved a farewell to Mr. Bergholc who had been our faithful interpreter for five weeks and two days.

Various ones told us that they were laboring under a severe strain at present in these parts, and that it was becoming even more difficult. During our visit we learned of the closing by the government of one of the churches for no legal offence. Mr. Peterson, the president of the R.E.E.M. Society, has since stated that some of these churches have been unmercifully closed, and the Christians are meeting in secret places to worship God. Every reader should pray for our compatriots of the heavenly kingdom laboring in these parts.

Chapter 14

UNDER THE SWASTIKA

WE arrived at the Free State border about six-thirty in the morning and proceeded to the city of Danzig. At the station platform we were met by a group of missionary friends and given a hearty welcome to the city. I received a grand surprise. Richard Bronson, a young man I met in Los Angeles, California, at the beginning of the present tour, has since received a definite call from God, and is now serving on the mission office staff in Danzig. It is truly a treat to meet a former friend in a far-away country. Arriving at the Bible school where the R.E.E.M. train all of their pastors and evangelsits, we found the students were standing in the vestibule vigorously singing a song of welcome.

Danzig is a very interesting city; it is old and has an unique history. Such brilliant fighters as Napoleon Bonaparte have waged war here. The free city of Danzig was severed from the German Reich by act of the Versailles Treaty on January 10, 1920. On November 15th it was declared an Independent Free State under the protection of the League of Nations.

Danzig has its own flag, heraldic arms and constitution. One does not tarry long here before feeling that freedom can be termed only in a restricted measure. After hearing the marching feet of a thousand men, and looking out of a window and seeing an officer leading his regiment, dressed in Nazi uniforms, wearing the swastika on their arms, and flying a Nazi flag in the front of the troops, he recognizes the influence of the Fuhrer.

We really saw more Nazi demonstrations in the Free State than in Berlin, the capital of Hitlerism. Two-thirds of the men and boys you saw meeting on the street, gave each other the Nazi salute of raised open hand with curved thumb. The greeting was "Heil Hitler." On Saturday and Sunday or a special holiday, you can look down a street with apartment houses on both sides and count twenty-five or more Nazi flags flying in one block from the windows. Nationalistic feeling runs to such extremes in Danzig at times, that the Nazis start a "free for all" fight with their opposers. Even in the elementary schools its influence is potent. Christian friends told us, because they would not permit their son to wear a Nazi uniform and swastika, the other boys at school tormented him incessantly. One night while here, a group of Nazi rowdies got outside the church and shouted to disturb the service.

Our stay in the Bible school was delightful. The students from different countries, speaking different languages, were very interesting. A teacher needs to be a linguist to be able to teach them all. The teacher gives all lessons in two languages, German and Russian, and then sometimes an unfortunate one has to have a fellow-student sit near to interpret. My early morning devotional chats, and Mr. Carter's Bible lessons were given through two interpreters. Through the unavoidable hindrance of language, the Holy Spirit came and anointed the teacher and the student, uniting them over God's Word. The students showed a keen perception of new truth and relished with delight the old truth presented in a new way. Some of the young men had not yet received the Pentecostal baptism, so Mr. Carter prayed with them, and two of them received the blessing.

The meetings in the mission hall were very encouraging, and the attendance was better than some had expected. The hall was nearly full for each service, and on Sunday night it was packed out, with people standing. A beautiful feature of the service was the excellent singing and the playing of stringed instruments. We could keenly feel the appreciation of the German Christians as they sat with rapt attention until two full sermons were preached. Many spoke of Mr. Carter's wonderful, deep, and spiritual Bible studies given each evening. When the plea was given for the un-converted, there were some who came forward to yield their all to the Lover of mankind. After ten days of precious fellowship, we boarded the midnight train for Germany.

We were now entering Berlin, one of Europe's largest and most glamorus cities. Just after daybreak we had crossed the Polish border into the German Reich. We were now in the heart of the European continent. After passing through the suburban district, and a few small stations, our express came to a halt at the great Schlesischer-Bahnhof station, where to our delight two German brethren were waiting for us. After hearty greetings, we were taken by electric car to the home where we were to stay. One ride through Berlin and the tremendous intensity of life and speed of a western nation could be felt and seen.

At this time, Berlin was preparing night and day for the great Olympic games. Great amphitheaters and stadia were being built, the airport was being enlarged fourfold, streets were being taken up and repaved, stores were displaying all kinds of goods with the Olympic insignia of five linked rings, representing the five continents. People of every color and country were invited to come and exhibit their prowess in sport to the world. Their aim was to bring about a more friendly relationship between the nations. On the opening day teams from more than fifty nations marched in under their national flag and took the Olympic oath of true comradeship. It is very strange that nations should seek comradeship on the basis of sport, when they are armed to the teeth and ready for the command to attack their so-called "comrades." True comradeship and permanent peace must have for their leader the Prince of Peace!

Semitic hatred could be detected with ease. We walked through municipal parks, by bathing pools and other places of public entertainment, and signs could be seen in predominating places, "No Jews allowed." "Through these gates does not lead to Palestine," "No dogs allowed," etc. Slogans used by the anti-semitic were such as these, "Sentimentality is high treason!" "People who trade at Jewish stores are traitors."

The brethren told us that permission had been obtained without difficulty from the Chief of Police for our visit, for which we praised God. Our first meeting was held the same evening of our arrival in Mr. Erbacker's church. From the beginning, we felt right at home in their midst. We were three nights in this church. Precious memories linger of the smiles and tears that were seen as Jesus Christ manifested himself in our midst. We were not at liberty to preach in different churches in Germany or Berlin. When we changed churches, a special permit had to be granted by the Chief

of Police. This was exacted of us to make it easy
for the Gestapo (Hitler's secret police) to sit in
the meetings and take notes on the sermon. It was
noticeable to us that when a strange person entered
the hall, the German Christians watched him with
a nervous eye, and a terrible depressing feeling
filled the church. Our sermons were restricted.
The interpreter had forewarned us not to speak in
strained tones, nor lift our voices unnecessarily.
He also asked us not preach about divine healing
or on the Holy Spirit, as the Nazis think these
things fanatical and would close the church. A
minister in Leipzig had been put in prison a few
days before for preaching that Christ could heal
human bodies today as he did two thousand years
ago. We do not know to what degree we were being
shadowed while in Germany, but we do know that
all our personal letters were officially opened and
resealed before we received them.

Further meetings were with the same pastor at
his church in another section of the city. Here we
found a lovely group of believers and a large
beautiful hall. The special music and singing
rendered by the local Christians was soul inspiring. On Good Friday we were invited to a Baptist
convention where a group of churches had rented
a large school auditorium. We were impressed by
the fervor of the ministers who spoke. The leader
was greatly moved by Mr. Carter's talk on our need

of the Holy Spirit. He told the congregation that what Germany needed in her churches was more of the Spirit of God. Our next and last meetings in the city were with Mr. Bartknecht. He gave up practicing law to pastor this church. These meetings were well attended, and the reserved German friends seemed to appreciate the hearty manner in which their foreign visitors ministered.

Easter Sunday was our farewell meeting day in Berlin. The morning service was glorious as the Christians were reminded of the greatness of our Lord's resurrection. In the evening the pastor whispered that a Gestapo agent was present. The detective's presence seemed to bind the liberty of the meeting, but after a time he got up and left, so our farewell meeting ended with blessing. We were requested by the German Christians to convey their sincere Christian greetings to other Christian bodies wherever God should send us.

Since leaving Germany, we have received letters and met one of the German pastors in New York State, who said the churches that we spoke in had been unmercifully closed by Hitler and padlocked, in his wild fight to place all churches under his direct supervision. The friends stated that there were no legal reasons given for their action. Some of the pastors have been placed in prison, others have been compelled to find secular work.

Chapter 15

SCANDINAVIA

AFTER spending two hours in Copenhagen, we boarded the Norwegian express and pulled out for Oslo, Norway. In an hour it crossed a ferry on to Swedish soil, and ran up the coastline all night. When we awoke the following morning, we were in the glorious land of the midnight sun. True to its name, we gazed upon scenes that were to be admired and remembered by anyone who appreciates Mother Nature at her best. Verdant mountains, towering into the hazy clouds, and beautiful valleys, whose mystic depths could hardly be seen at all, passed us in kaleidoscopic grandeur. Large sawmills were passed with logs floating lazily about the pond waiting to be dragged up a chain and sawn, dried and dressed, then sent to different countries and cities to serve its useful purpose.

It was all so entrancing that it seemed only a few moments until the magnificent harbor of Oslo could be sighted and its large buildings, towering above the busy streets, plainly visible.

What a welcome! Mr. Barrett, the venerable apostle of Pentecost in Norway and many places on the continent, was down to welcome us as his guests. He had invited Mr. Carter and myself to conduct special meetings in his great Filadelfia Church, (church of brotherly love), which is the largest auditorium, and has the greatest attendance of any place of worship in Norway. He has over 2,500 members on his charter roll. Since we were there, this church building has burned, and now he is constructing a larger one, as the old one was always packed full with a few hundred standing. A great crowd greeted us in our first meeting that evening, in Filadelfia Temple. Mr. Carter conveyed greetings from the homeland and from other Christian churches in the countries and cities we had visited. At the close of the first service a few precious souls were won for Christ.

One of the greatest things that impressed us in Scandinavia was the sincere courtesy and etiquette of the people. When a young girl meets you she always makes a charming curtsy. The boys shook hands and bowed their heads slightly.

On the second day in Oslo there were two meetings. The morning one was specially for the the Christians. Brother Carter opened up for them some hidden gems from his basket. In the evening the auditorium and the gallery were packed and many were standing. After the lovely choir and well trained orchestra had rendered a beautiful preliminary, the Lord anointed His Word as it went forth, and a number of souls yielded to Christ.

One morning Brother Barrett took a few friends, and ourselves, up on the mountains that stand guard over beautiful Oslo for breakfast. The feast was true Norwegian style, salads, pickled mackerel, etc. all cold, for breakfast! From here a superb panorama of the famous islet-dotted fjords held one spellbound.

The noonday services, which were intended at first to be held three days during the week, were held every day. The great hall would be two-thirds full of believers, hungry for the precious truths. These meetings were simply glorious, the Lord's presence brought tears and then a holy laughter, and again psalms of praise and hallelujahs. It seemed that the glory that inspired David to dance before the Lord was in our midst. On Friday night a beautiful baptismal service was held in the Temple. Seven followed the Lord in Christian baptism.

A visit was paid on Saturday afternoon to the city of Dammen, fifty kilometers from Oslo. The meeting was splendid, and the hall, seating over 600, was packed full. Though it was snowing outside, there was a very warm spirit inside. Sunday, our last day, was full of blessing. In the morning the hall was full of Christians, and the Holy

Spirit made the Savior very real to all of us. The largest crowd of the week gathered in the evening, filling the church to suffocation, with many standing on the outside. Blessing flowed in streams. The acme was reached when the unconverted were led to the feet of their Lord.

The farewell meeting was one long to be remembered. It only passed to quickly, bringing to a close our lovely, and long to be remembered, visit to Norway.

Next day we stopped at the border town separating Norway and Sweden. Some immigration officers boarded the train to stamp an immigration permit in our passports. Then the train pulled across the border into beautiful Sweden.

It was interesting for us to learn that these peaceful Scandinavians (Norway and Sweden) made a peace pact over 200 years ago and placed a memorial stone on the border to hold their truce in remembrance. Since, they have been neighbors with an unbroken friendship. A treaty with that amount of sincerity and number of peaceful years in it is worth remembering. Our train circled around a few waterways, over a bridge and came to a halt at the Stockholm central station. We were soon in the private office of Pastor Pethrus in Filadelfia Church. Here three press photographers and four press correspondents were busy eliciting information from two weary visitors.

Great interest is manifested in Sweden concerning the "Church of the Filadelfia." In the last twenty-five years it has grown from obscurity into the limelight. It has about 6,000 members, everyone having been baptized in water, and the majority of them filled with the Holy Spirit. The church has a seating capacity of some 4,000, and while we were there, the architect was drawing plans to enlarge it another thousand, as hundreds of people are often turned away. The pastor informed us that, speaking generally, tourists visit Stockholm to see three structures—the King's palace, the parliament buildings and the Filadelfia church. A hinder section of the temple is the famous and historic Rorstrand Castle. This church reaps a greater attendance than any theater, picture palace or church in the whole nation of Sweden! There has been a continuous revival fire burning these many years which totals an average of 30 decisions a week for Christ. Praise God for the reality of the Gospel.

The marvelous consecrated talent found in Filadelfia Church is worth noting. Its founder and pastor, whose person makes one feel he has met one of God's mighty men, is Mr. Lewi Pethrus. A friend whispered in my ear that he was one of Sweden's outstanding religious orators. His spiritual influence throughout the land is potential. Mr. Widmen, the editor of the church paper, is one of Sweden's greatest writers. He has taken national prizes several times. A friend said he was recognized as the man with the greatest Swedish vocabulary. His success has won him an audience with the King. Mr. Svedlund, the pianist of the church, is nationally and internationally known as a master of music. Mr. Einar Ekberg, the premier soloist for the church, is considered to have one of the finest voices in Europe. In this marvelous church God has placed men and women of talent and consecration. Brother Pethrus remarked that one of the strongest reasons for the great influence and phenomenal growth of the work of God in Sweden was the deep sincerity and holy lives of its adherents. May God help the Christian world to follow such an example. The Filadelfia Church also has a marvelous missionary vision. The Stockholm assembly fully supports over 30 missionaries and partly supports ten others, while the Swedish work as a whole has some 200 workers on the foreign field.

Our visit to Stockholm was one never to be forgotten. The fellowship and blessing were such that it made us know we were brethren. The pastor invited us to be there during the annual week of Bible Study, when visiting pastors and evangelists from all parts of Sweden were present, and also a number of foreign missionaries. We were happy to meet Brother Landin, whom we had labored with in Peiping, North China. There were two meetings each day, which were loaded with blessings from the heavenly storehouse. Mr. Carter gave Bible lessons to the ministers and Christians. It was here that a severe attack of malaria seized Mr. Carter's body. They came twice daily, accompanied by terrible ague and high fever, but, thanks be to God, he had sufficient strength to attend every service except one. At our last meeting in Stockholm on Monday evening, the Lord's supper was celebrated. The writer never remembers having seen a sight like it before—the enormous quantity of bread (layer upon layer) and there appeared to some gallons of wine in the shining silver cups. The great temple was filled with the glory of God. At the close of the meeting, the assembly stood to express their appreciation for our visit and asked us to convey their heartiest greetings to all like-minded believers throughout the world.

The following morning we boarded the train, traveling most of the day through beautiful Swedish scenery to Halsingborg, on the Baltic coast. Here we spent one night and ministered in the beautiful Smyrna church. The newly built auditorium, seating about 700, was filled. The Lord was present in a precious way, and blessed the gathering.

The next morning, as we steamed out across the Baltic Sea, I saw my last of the flaxen haired

Swedes, whose kindness rouses a desire in one's heart to return to their land again.

Our train pulled into Copenhagen, the peninsular city, which is nearly surrounded by water. Now we were to minister a few days in the capital city of the great Danes.

Mr. Jensen, a former student of Hampstead Bible School, London, met us at the station. His being here was a great surprise to us, as he was laboring in far distant Yunnan, China, as a missionary when we were there. He was our interpreter while in Copenhagen. We were taken from the station to the meeting hall for the first service. When we arrived, a good number of Christians had gathered for a Bible study. In the evening the beautiful hall, which is situated in the center of the business district and seats between seven and eight hundred, was a scene of revival and blessing. The Danes do not have as demonstrative a nature as we Americans, but there is an appreciation which can be felt.

Our few days' visit to Copenhagen was very delightful. We were happy to add their acquaintance to our ever-growing list of countries. The meetings were primarily held for the edifying of the saints. The attendance continued to grow each day until the end. A few sinners surrendered their broken lives to the Great Repairer, and they left the church rejoicing in a newly found Savior. The

Danish missionary zeal is apparent when we learned from one pastor that more missionaries were supported on the foreign fields than there were evangelists in the home work.

Our happy days of fellowship ended. Mr. Carter took an airplane to London for a special business conference. I traveled with a friend across the island to the Danish mainland and preached in Aarhus in the evening, then proceeded overland to Amsterdam, Holland, where we were to meet again.

Chapter 16

HOMEWARD BOUND

WE were taught at school that one half of the whole of Holland is below sea level, and that all its important cities are built on millions of piles. All of Amsterdam is built on piling, even the great union station where I arrived. It is said that there are 14,000 under the Royal Palace in Amsterdam alone.

For two days we ministered in Amsterdam. The meetings were well attended. From here we took the electric train down to Rotterdam. School days and geography loomed up before me as we saw the solemn windmills move slowly by the wind, or a dog pulling a cart, cows grazing in the meadows wearing a nice sackcloth suit of clothes to keep them from getting chilled. The whole country was flat but fresh and green with grass and flowers.

Arriving in Rotterdam, we were met by Mr. Van Der Woude, our host while here, and pastor of the church in which we were to minister. Rotterdam is a very interesting place. Like Amsterdam, it is built on piles. It is Holland's second city in size and commercial importance. We thought it quaint for them to have a drawbridge in the middle of the city, across a large canal. Every time we went to town it was up, letting a boat through, holding up the traffic a few minutes. The two meetings here were especially blessed. A revival atmosphere was present, and a good number decided definitely to live for our loving Savior.

Leaving Rotterdam, we went to Sassenheim, situated in the center of bulbland. We arrived just in time to behold a sight worth much traveling to see. As far as the eyes could scan, beautiful patches of flaming colored tulips could be seen. The country was garlanded with inconceivable beauty. A network of canals ran like silver threads through them. In Sassenheim we ministered twice, the Lord confirming His Word with signs following.

Here one of Mr. Carter's attacks of malaria came on him when traveling. Therefore we deemed it wise to cancel our engagements in Belgium, France and Switzerland, and go direct to London.

Arriving at the Rotterdam airport we purchased tickets, and bade our kind Dutch friends farewell. The engine roared madly and the whole plane trembled. We moved slowly down the runway. Our friends became small, the aerodrome came into minature and then Rotterdam canals looked like crooked lines drawn on a bas-relief map. We headed straight for the Hook of Holland and across the North Sea toward Harwich, England.

Thus ended a tour around the world by faith in God. As Mr. Carter aptly said, "We started with nothing, we had nothing (i.e. no surplus), we returned with nothing, and we desire nothing, but the privilege of proclaiming the glad news that 'Hallelujah, our Lord God Omnipotent Reigneth!' "

The Lord be magnified in all things.

Other books by Lester Sumrall:

- My Story To His Glory
- Take It—It's Yours
- Gifts & Ministries Of The Holy Spirit
- Alien Entities
- Battle Of The Ages
- Conscience—The Scales Of Eternal Justice
- Demons The Answer Book
- Bitten By Devils
- Ecstasy—Finding Joy In Living
- Faith To Change The World
- Faith Under Siege; The Life of Abraham
- Fishers Of Men
- Gates Of Hell
- Genesis—Crucible Of The Universe
- Hostility
- Hypnotism—Divine Or Demonic
- Imagination—Hidden Force Of Human Potential
- I Predict 2000 A.D.
- Jerusalem, Where Empires Die—
        Will America Die At Jerusalem?
- Jihad—The Holy War
- Living Free
- Making Life Count
- Miracles Don't Just Happen
- 101 Questions & Answers On Demon Power
- Paul—Man Of The Millennia
- Run With The Vision
- Secrets Of Answered Prayer
- Sixty Things God Said About Sex
- Supernatural Principalities & Powers
- 20 Years Of "I Predict"
- The Battle Of The Ages
- The Making Of A Champion
- The Names Of God
- The Reality Of Angels
- The Stigma Of Calvary
- The Total Man
- The Will—The Potent Force Of The Universe
- The Human Body
- The Human Soul
- The Human Spirit
- Trajectory Of Faith—Joseph
- Unprovoked Murder
- You Can Conquer GRIEF Before It Conquers You
- Miracles And The Sumrall Family
  (by Leona Sumrall Murphy)
- The Marriage Triangle (Leona Sumrall Murphy)

World Harvest Magazine has been published since April of 1962. It has been
Dr. Lester Sumrall's pulpit to the world,
each issue containing faith-building
articles and up-dates of what God is doing
through LeSEA Ministries. You may have
a free copy by writing:

LeSEA, INC.,
P.O. Box 12, South Bend Indiana 46624.
24 Hour Prayerline - (219) 291-1010